Weaving Freeform
Wire Jewelry

Step-by-step techniques, 20 versatile designs

Kaska Firor

KALMBACH BOOKS

*To my mom
and dad*

Kalmbach Books
21027 Crossroads Circle
Waukesha, Wisconsin 53186
www.Kalmbach.com/Books

© 2014 Kaska Firor

Lettered step-by-step photos by the author. All other photography © 2014 Kalmbach Books except where otherwise noted.

Please follow appropriate health and safety measures when working with materials and equipment. Some general guidelines are presented in this book, but always read and follow manufacturers' instructions.

Published in 2014
18 17 16 15 14   1 2 3 4 5

Manufactured in the United States of America

ISBN: 978-0-87116-703-3
EISBN: 978-1-62700-087-1

Editor: Erica Swanson
Art Director: Lisa Bergman
Technical Editor: Hazel Wheaton
Layout Designer: Lisa Schroeder
Photographers: James Forbes, William Zuback

Publisher's Cataloging-in-Publication Data

Firor, Kaska.
   Weaving freeform wire jewelry : step-by-step techniques, 20 versatile designs / Kaska Firor.

   p. : col. ill. ; cm.

   Issued also as an ebook.
   ISBN: 978-0-87116-703-3

   1. Wire jewelry—Handbooks, manuals, etc. 2. Wire jewelry—Patterns. 3. Jewelry making—Handbooks, manuals, etc. 4. Metal-work—Handbooks, manuals, etc. 5. Weaving—Handbooks, manuals, etc. I. Title.

TT212 .F57 2014
745.594/2

Table of Contents

Introduction

I was drawn to handicrafts from the time I was little. As a child, I built things out of found objects. Acorns and buckeyes joined with matchsticks in my hands to become figurines of horses and people. I strung forest berries and nuts into necklaces and bracelets, and braided wild flowers into tiaras. During long summer vacations, my brother and I roamed the woods at our family friends' farm, making whistles out of fresh willow switches, carving relief designs into walking sticks, and building houses with walls made of intertwined tree branches.

As I got older and became fond of more tools, my passion for working with my hands and making things continued. In college, I chose to study interior design, but I kept getting pulled toward more hands-on endeavors. Over the years I have tried bronze casting, clay sculpture, creative sawing, stained glass, and more.

Then in the summer of 2000, I took my first class in wire jewelry. I fell in love with it immediately! From the moment I picked up my first pair of pliers and started manipulating the wire, I knew I had arrived at a comfortable and somehow familiar place.

My initial venture into wire media was traditional wire-wrapping. I spent several happy years learning and improving my wire skills, and I had a lot of fun experimenting with and pushing the limits of that art form. Still, all along, my capricious nature kept me longing for something more spontaneous and unpredictable than wire-wrapping provided, and when I came across freeform wire weaving, I was instantly hooked.

From the very beginning, I loved that I didn't always have to know what the finished piece would look like. I liked how the unique interplay of frames and weaving wires, the two building blocks of freeform weaving, made alterations and additions possible at almost any phase of the design—and how I could change the project's direction in mid-process and end up with something unexpected, even to myself.

As I ventured further into the world of freeform weaving, I discovered how versatile and flexible this art form truly is. The variety of different two- and three-dimensional shapes that are possible with freeform weaving is quite remarkable. From angular, geometric forms to organic, curvy, elongated lines, and from simple flat weaves to elaborate multi-layered creations, there seems to be no end to the options.

There are many different ways to incorporate beads, cabochons, stones, and other elements into the woven designs, which makes freeform weaving incredibly adaptable. Techniques such as incorporating beads directly into the weaves or stitching them onto the surfaces of woven sections, creating coiled, looped, or woven bezels to hold cabochons, and building three-dimensional vessels to cradle diversely shaped stones are just some of the many choices you'll find in this book.

The endless assortment of contrasting patterns of the weaves is still another aspect of freeform weaving that allows for a wide range of design options. To weave is to create textures. Even though each weave type has its own unique pattern, you can generate infinite number of variations by mixing different weaves, by adjusting the number and sizes of wires, and by changing directions and alternating compactness of the weaves. The resulting juxtaposition of different weaves creates beautifully sculpted surfaces that shimmer in the light, giving woven jewelry a distinctive look that is a feast for the eyes.

Freeform wire weaving can often be unpredictable and unruly. In contrast, it can also be extremely structured and organized, as demonstrated by some of the very precisely designed projects in this book. Jewelry crafted with freeform weaving techniques can be light and elegant, dark and mysterious, or anything in between. It can be worn by the most sophisticated bride, or be a part of a casual jeans-and-T-shirt outfit. Freeform weaving's flexible nature makes it adaptable to each person's individual taste, potentially resulting in as many freeform weaving styles as there are wire-weaving artists.

"From angular, geometric forms to organic, curvy, elongated lines, and from simple flat weaves to elaborate multi-layered creations, there seems to be no end to the options."

I tried to infuse this book with the enthusiasm and passion I feel for the art of wire weaving, hoping it will be contagious and that you, too, will catch the fever. If you are new to the wire arts, freeform wire weaving is an excellent place to start. Welcome! If you are a wire-wrapping artist venturing out in search of something new and different, you will most likely find these techniques exciting and liberating. And, if you are already familiar with freeform wire weaving, I hope this book will provide you with some fresh ideas and help to spark your creativity.

Enjoy the adventure!

—*Kaska*

Basics

Before diving into wire-weaving techniques, it is important to understand the basic properties of the materials and tools you will be using to create weaving projects. This section will give you a brief introduction to these materials and tools, as well as a guide to several techniques used in preparing frame wires for weaving, tips for more successful weaving, and simple instructions for applying finishing touches to your designs.

About Wire

Whether you work with wire only, or incorporate other elements such as beads, stones, or cabochons into your woven design, wire is the component that will have the greatest impact on that piece. After all, there would be no wire weaving without the wire! For that reason, it's important to know about the various types of wire—different shapes, sizes, and metals—as well as their properties and design applications.

Frame and Weaving Wires

Throughout the book I will be using the terms **frame wire** and **weaving wire**. These terms describe the different tasks that each wire type is assigned. Frame wires are used to create the overall outline of a piece of jewelry. During the weaving process, they remain mostly stationary while the weaving wires move around them, stitching all the parts together to create various patterns and give the design stability. Frame wires are like bricks in a masonry construction, whereas weaving wire is like the mortar. Although each has a different function, both work together to form a cohesive unit, and one could not do its job properly without the other. When woven jewelry is designed well and crafted skillfully, it should be strong and have a solid feel to it.

Selecting Wire

As with any functional art, there are two facets to jewelry design: the aesthetic, which has to do with the sensual expression of the art, and the practical, which deals with the construction of the piece and its functionality, strength, and comfort to the wearer.

When selecting wire for your project, it is helpful to understand how different wire properties can impact one or both of these equally important design aspects. For example, choosing the wire's color and metal type is almost entirely an aesthetic decision, and choosing the degree of wire's hardness will be purely a functional one. When deciding what sizes or shapes of wires to use, you will have to consider both the aesthetic and the practical impact of that choice on your design.

Wire Shapes

Even though everyone is most familiar with round wire, wire is also available in several other shapes. Square, half-round, domed, rectangular, and triangular wires are often used in wire wrapping and other jewelry-making techniques.

Round wire offers the greatest versatility, and it is still the most frequently used shape of wire in both jewelry and non-jewelry applications. Round wire is available in the widest array of colors, sizes, and types of metals. Also, and most importantly: Because of its shape, round wire bends with equal ease in all directions, which makes it the easiest to mold into various configurations. This property is very important in freeform weaving designs that require a lot of bending and frequent changes in direction, so you will find that most freeform wire weaving and the majority of projects in this book are designed with round wire only.

Square wire has four flat sides and four corners. The gauge of square wire is determined by its thickness, the same as round wire. However, because its corners add extra bulk, square wire has about 20% more metal in it than round wire of the same size. Square wire bends most easily and cleanly along one of its flat sides. When working with square wire, be careful not to turn it the wrong way and end up with a twist where it does not belong. Square wire can be used to make twisted wire to use as accents. (Be aware that twisting hardens the wire.)

Half-round wire has one flat and one rounded side. Its gauge is determined by its width, and because it is half of a round wire, its weight is also half of round wire of the same gauge. It bends well only toward the flat side. Half-round wire is commonly used in wire wrapping to bind square or round wires together. In weaving projects, it can be used for the same purpose. In addition, it can be used to add decorative elements to woven work. For example, you can wrap half-round wire around a frame wire to create slightly different coiling effects than you get when using round wire. The heavier gauges can also be used as frame wires in some limited applications.

Triangular and **low-dome** wires only come in large gauges and are not suitable for use in freeform weaving.

Wire Hardness

Precious metal wires such as gold, gold-filled, fine silver, sterling silver, and Argentium sterling silver, are sold in three degrees of hardness, or stiffness: **hard**, **half hard,** and **dead soft**. Brass, bronze, and copper wires are usually available only in dead soft. Color-coated copper, anodized aluminum, and other artistic and craft wires are sold in various degrees of hardness that is often unspecified and differs from manufacturer to manufacturer. Experiment a bit with different brands to see which ones work best for you.

Keep in mind that hardness designation such as "dead soft" does not mean that all types of wires with that label will be exactly the same degree of firmness. For example: dead-soft sterling silver wire is slightly harder than dead-soft copper wire, and brass and bronze wires are even stiffer.

There are also methods for changing the degree of hardness of wire, such as annealing it with a torch or in a kiln to soften it, or work-hardening it by drawing it through a drawplate or striking it repeatedly with a plastic or rawhide hammer.

Selecting which hardness of wire to use for your project is a purely practical decision.

Weaving wire

Since weaving wire's job requires it to bend and twist into tight curves and loops, it needs to be as malleable as possible, and therefore it should always be dead-soft. Be aware that your wire will work-harden (or become stiffer) during weaving, which is another reason to start with the softest wire possible. You will know the wire is soft enough when it bends effortlessly into graceful curves and follows the flow of the weave. In contrast, when it bends in all the wrong places and breaks easily, it is probably too firm and will most likely result in a jagged, uneven weave.

Fine-silver and copper wires—including some color-coated copper—are the softest and easiest to use. Dead-soft wires such as sterling silver, Argentium sterling, gold-filled, and gold also work very well.

Frame wire

Selecting the right firmness for the frame wires is a little more complicated than for the weaving wires. In most cases, neither the soft nor the hard wire is an ideal choice. Hard wire holds its shape much better, both during the weaving process and later in the finished jewelry; however, it can be difficult to manipulate and once formed, it is almost impossible to reshape without leaving unsightly bumps and nicks. Soft wire, on the other hand, is great for forming curves and loops and is fairly easy to reshape if something needs to be readjusted. At the same time, because it is soft, it tends to

Wire gauge chart

AWG	in.	mm
31	.009	.23
30	.010	.25
29	.011	.29
28	.013	.33
27	.014	.36
26	.016	.40
25	.018	.46
24	.020	.50
23	.023	.57
22	.025	.65
21	.028	.72
20	.032	.80
19	.036	.91
18	.040	1.00
17	.045	1.15
16	.051	1.30
15	.057	1.45
14	.064	1.60

SWG	in.	mm
33	0.010	0.25
32	0.011	0.27
31	0.012	0.29
30	0.013	0.32
29	0.014	0.35
28	0.015	0.38
27	0.016	0.42
26	0.018	0.46
25	0.020	0.51
24	0.022	0.56
23	0.024	0.610
22	0.028	0.711
21	0.032	0.813
20	0.036	0.914
19	0.040	1.016
18	0.048	1.219
17	0.056	1.422
16	0.064	1.626

get distorted during weaving. Jewelry pieces created with dead-soft wire often need to be tumbled for a long time to make them strong.

Because of the way I usually work, designing as I weave and changing things along the way, I tend to reach for dead-soft wire most often. However, there are some applications where dead-soft wire will not work at all. As you get familiar with the weaving techniques and become more experienced with using wire, you will develop your own sense of which wire hardness to use and when.

Here are some basic guidelines I use when selecting frame wires' firmness.

For:

- **geometric shapes requiring precise, sharp angles and rigid sides:** Use all half-hard wire.
- **parallel ribbons that will be used flat:** Use all half-hard wire or both half-hard and dead-soft wire.
- **ribbons that will be braided or twisted after being woven:** Use all dead-soft wire; you can add one half-hard wire for extra stability.
- **flat shapes:** Use half-hard wire with small gauges, and use dead-soft wire with large gauges and small shapes.
- **filigree work:** Use half-hard wire for the outside frame, dead-soft wire for all filigree shapes.
- **wires shaped prior to being woven, such as when working with a template:** Use dead-soft wire and then harden it by hammering with a hammer prior to weaving.
- **coiling:** Use all dead-soft wire.

NOTE:
Full-hard wire is very hard and extremely difficult to bend; therefore, it is reserved for specific applications, such as brooch pins. It is rarely used for weaving.

Wire Size (Gauge)

All jewelry wire and other nonferrous metal wire (meaning that it contains no iron) such as silver, gold, copper, brass, and bronze is sold in sizes measured in gauges or millimeters. The American Wire Gauge (AWG), also known as Brown and Sharpe (B&S), is the system used almost universally in the United States and Canada. Standard Wire Gauge (SWG), or British Standard, is used in the United Kingdom and sometimes in Canada. In Europe, wire is measured mostly in millimeters. When purchasing wire, you should always check to see what measuring system has been used. This is especially important when buying wire not specifically made for jewelry and wire purchased from outside of the U.S. All gauge indications in this book refer to AWG standard.

In both gauge-measuring systems, the smaller the gauge number, the thicker the wire. For example, 14 gauge will be thicker than 20 gauge. If you have not worked with wire before, this concept may be a bit confusing at first—but you will get used to it fairly quickly.

AWG sizes range from thinner than hair (40 gauge) to as thick as a child's finger (0000 gauge). Even though there is no strict rule as to what thicknesses of wire to use for weaving—you could use any and all gauges available if you chose to—most freeform weaving is designed with fairly limited mid-range wire sizes. The reason for this is mostly practical; the very thin wires break too easily, and the very thick ones are too hard to bend and are too heavy for jewelry-design applications. For this book, I've used 20, 18, and 16 gauges for the frame wires, and 30, 28, and 26 gauge for the weaving wires.

Since it will affect both the aesthetic and the practical aspects of your design, the selection of wire gauges is one of the most important decisions you will make.

Practical considerations

Pliability: It is important that the gauge of the wire you select will be able to be shaped according to the design's requirements. Thinner wire is more bendable and can be shaped into intricate patterns more easily than thicker wire. For example, if you will need to form very small components with tight bends in them, 14 gauge will probably not be a good choice.

Frame wire to weaving wire ratio: The gauge of weaving wire will depend in part on the size of frame wire being used. To start with, the frame wire needs to be quite a bit thicker than the weaving wire in order for it to hold its shape when being pulled at during the weaving process. For instance, it would be very difficult to use 24-gauge frame wire with 26-gauge weaving wire. At the same time, the weaving wire cannot be too thin, or it may be too weak to hold together the much heavier frame wires. Generally, the thicker the frame wires, the thicker the weaving wire needs to be.

Some good frame wire/weaving wire combinations are:

16 gauge/26 gauge

18 gauge/26 gauge

18 gauge/28 gauge

20 gauge/26 gauge

20 gauge/28 gauge

20 gauge/30 gauge

22 gauge/28 gauge

22 gauge/30 gauge

Weight: Since jewelry is meant to be worn, its finished weight must always be taken into consideration during the design process. Wire is a solid metal, and a piece designed with several strips of 16- or 18-gauge wires all woven together can become quite heavy. Ask yourself these questions:

- **What am I designing?** Earrings have to be lighter than a necklace or a bracelet.
- **Who is going to wear it?** Generally, jewelry for men can be heavier than jewelry for women or children.
- **What beads and/or stones am I using in my design?** If your design calls for a lot of beads or large stones, consider using thinner frame wires to reduce the weight of the piece.

Artistic considerations

In addition to practical considerations, the sizes of wires selected for a particular design will also have a significant impact on its overall artistic expression. Weaves created with thinner wires, such as 20, 30, and 28 gauge, will produce fine, uniform textures, resulting in delicate, elegant pieces. In contrast, similar designs crafted with heavier 16-, 18-, and 26-gauge wires will result in a much bolder appearance.

Combining several different wire sizes is another way to vary the outcome. For example, a piece of jewelry designed with all 20-gauge frame wires will look quite bit different when you replace even just one of these wires with 16 or 14 gauge.

The ratio of frame to weaving wires is another factor that can be manipulated to influence the appearance of a piece of woven jewelry. For instance, a 20- and 28-gauge wire combination will have a very different look than a 16- and 28-gauge combination.

Metals and Colors

Wire is available in a wide range of metals and colors. Aside from considerations such as the price of a particular wire or its availability in a certain gauge or hardness, these wire characteristics will impact the artistic expression of a design only—not its practical performance.

Metals such as 24k gold, fine silver, and copper are considered pure metals (99.9%) and have their own inherent colors. Combining these metals with other elements during the manufacturing process creates alloys such as bronze, lower karat gold, brass, and sterling silver. By manipulating the combinations and percentages of the elements in an alloy, you can alter the colors (that is how copper combined with tin becomes bronze, for example). A lot of color tweaking is done with gold, resulting in gold shades of red, green, pink, and even blue and purple. Solid-metal wire made of any of these metals has color that goes all the way through.

Other wires, such as gold and silver-filled, craft wires, coated copper wires, and many others, have a thin layer of color applied to the outside surface of base wire. These wires are widely available in many different colors from subtle pastels to bright primary hues to loud neon shades.

Color is a very powerful design tool that can be used to create many different effects. Most artists develop their own color preferences. I like the subtle shades of gold, silver, copper, brass, and bronze. The plainness of these metals allows the beautiful textures of the weaves to stand on their own and be artistic expressions by themselves, or serve as a background to the more colorful stones and beads. As a bonus, these wires can be hammered, textured, and melted with a torch to form balled ends. I use these techniques in most of my designs, and they are not advisable with coated, filled, or plated wires.

With one exception (the Heart of Gold Pendant, which was made from gold-filled wire), all projects in this book were crafted using solid metal wires. However, feel free to substitute any and all of these wires for the materials and colors that better suit your own artistic vision.

Metal types

Fine silver is 99.9% pure silver. It is extremely soft, making it ideal for use as weaving wire. Also, since it doesn't develop firescale, fine silver doesn't need to be cleaned after being heated (as when balling up the wire ends). Jewelry constructed with fine silver alone usually needs to be tumbled for a few hours to be hardened.

Sterling silver is an alloy of 92.5% fine silver and 7.5% copper. It is stronger than fine silver and holds its shape.

Argentium sterling silver is an alloy of fine silver, copper, and germanium. The addition of germanium makes the silver resistant to firescale and tarnish, which is very desirable to those that prefer their jewelry to remain shiny. Do not use Argentium sterling silver if you are planning to finish your piece with liver of sulfur.

Silver-filled wire is made with a solid layer of sterling silver bonded to base metal (usually brass) with heat and pressure. Silver-filled wire is often designated 1/10 or 1/20, meaning that either 10% or 5% (respectively) of the total weight of the wire is silver. Keep in mind that the yellow brass core of the wire will show at the cut ends.

24k gold is considered pure (99.9%) gold. Lower-karat golds are alloys of gold and other elements. The element the gold is combined with determines the alloy's color. For example: Adding copper to pure gold creates red gold, adding silver to gold makes green gold, and combining different percentages of aluminum with gold will result in purple or blue gold. The amount of pure gold in an alloy delineates its karat or purity. For example, 18k gold is 18 parts pure gold and six parts other metals, and 14k is 14 parts gold and 10 parts other metals. The parts always add up to 24.

Gold-filled wire is made with solid layer of a karated gold bonded to base metal (usually brass). Most gold-filled wire is made with 14k gold and has a designation of 14/20, which means that the amount of the 14k gold by weight is at least 1/20 (5%) of the total weight of the wire. The gold layer in most gold-filled wires is very durable, so gold-filled wire is a good alternative to using expensive solid gold.

Brass is an alloy of copper and zinc, has a yellow color similar to gold, and is resistant to tarnish. Brass wire is a little stiffer than copper and silver, but it is still very malleable, making it a good choice for weaving.

Copper is pure metal that is very soft in its natural state. It is an excellent choice for weaving wire, but it is often too soft for frame wires. Consider using bronze as a substitute when half-hard wire is required.

Bronze, sometimes referred to as red brass because of its reddish-gold color, is an alloy of copper and tin. Bronze is stiffer than copper but softer than brass. It works great as a substitute for copper when half-hard frame wires are required.

Nickel silver, also known as **German** or **new silver**, is an alloy of copper, nickel, and sometimes zinc. It has a very shiny silver appearance and does not tarnish. Despite its name, nickel silver contains no actual silver.

Color-enameled copper is made by coating pure copper wire with several layers of enamel color, a process that makes the color very durable and scratch-resistant. Enameled copper wires are generally as soft as pure copper wires. They are available in many different colors and are a great choice if you want to add some brilliant color to your designs.

Silver-plated enameled copper is similar to color-enameled copper with an addition of silver plating under the colored enamel. The silver plating makes the colors more vivid and shiny.

Other Materials

Beads

A bead is any object that has a hole through it that can be used as an embellishment in a jewelry design. There are countless varieties of beads available today. There are beads in any shape and finish you can imagine. They come in sizes from tiny 1mm seed beads to huge 40–50mm focal beads. They are made from precious and semi-precious stones, clay, porcelain, glass, bone, wood, acrylic, horn, coral, shell, metal, and more. Many beads are machine-made in factories; others are individually hand-cut, sculpted, and lampworked. Select beads that you find beautiful and interesting that inspire your creativity.

Stones

Just like beads, stones come in a mind-spinning assortment of colors and patterns. You can purchase these from jewelry supply, rock and mineral, and bead stores. If you purchase your stones directly from a stone cutter or lapidary artist, he or she may be able to custom-cut them to your specifications.

Tumbled stones are usually smooth rocks that have been polished by a mechanical tumbler or a natural tumbling process in a river or ocean.

Natural crystals are transparent or translucent stones whose shapes have not been altered by human hand (for example, quartz, citrine, and amethyst).

Cabochons are stones that are domed on one side and flat on the other. They come in many different shapes and sizes and are usually (but not always) symmetrical. Some art glass and ceramics are also made into cabochons, and flat beach or river stones can be used.

Embellishments

You can use practically anything to embellish your woven designs: found objects, fossils, shells, sea glass, etc. Treat each one of these elements the same way you would a bead, a stone, or a cabochon.

Findings

Findings are the functional design elements, such as clasps, ear wires, chains, cords, brooch pins, jump rings, and headpins, that are used to connect and hang jewelry elements. There are many commercially available findings that you can purchase at bead shops, at bead shows, and online. You can also create many findings yourself.

Make sure your findings complement your woven designs well. Often findings are an afterthought, considered only when the design is completed or nearly completed. Make them part of the design process from the beginning.

Use woven crescents, gemstone drops, and decorative headpins to create a stunning pair of earrings.

Tools and Supplies

Freeform weaving can be done mostly with your hands. All you really need is a good pair of wire cutters and a pair of chainnose pliers, and you are on the way to many years of happy weaving. To me, using tools is part of the joy of jewelry making, so the right tools make various tasks easier, and some techniques would not be possible without them.

Buy the best tools you can afford; it will pay off in the long run. The most important tools for wire weaving are listed under "weaving tools," especially cutters and pliers, which you will be using all the time; make sure these are of good quality. The best way to choose your tools is to handle them before buying. Tools that are right for you should feel good in your hand and perform like a natural extension of your body.

Weaving Tools

You should have two pairs of **wire cutters**: one for cutting weaving wire, and one for frame wires. The weaving-wire cutters should have a small head with very sharp and pointy cutting tips that can get into tight spaces. These do not have to be very powerful, since you will be using them only to cut thin weaving wire. (To avoid damaging their fine cutting edges, do not use these for snipping the large-gauge frame wires.) For cutting frame wires, use heavy-duty flush cutters that can cut up to 14-gauge wire. These should not be too expensive, because they will get dull and have to be replaced pretty often, especially if you cut a lot of large-gauge brass and bronze wire.

Flatnose, roundnose, and chainnose (or needlenose) pliers are used for manipulating and shaping frame wires. Flatnose pliers should have squared jaws with sharp edges that can be used for bending wire. Roundnose pliers should have evenly tapered, round conical barrels with very small tips. Chainnose (or needlenose) pliers' tips should come to a fine point (about 1mm or smaller each). Chainnose pliers are also great for pulling weaving wires through tight spaces. All pliers should have smooth (non-serrated) jaws that won't mar the wire.

When working with hair-thin wire, it is nice to have either a **visor** or **magnifying lamp** (at least 5X magnification). Even if your eyesight is excellent and you choose to work without a magnification device, you will be thankful you have one handy when your wires get twisted or you make a mistake and have to figure out which end goes where in a tangle of tiny wires.

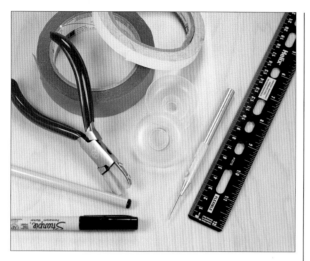

By far my favorite, a simple **needle tool** is a long, needle-like pointed tip with a handle. I use it for manipulating, lifting, guiding, and separating weaving wires, as well as for making spaces between weaves for stitching. It is very helpful when working in tight spaces and as an aid in the finishing process to tuck in loose ends and attach beads.

Nylon-jaw pliers are great for grasping elements that have already been woven. The soft jaws will not flatten or damage the weaving wires.

Use a **wooden dowel or plastic pen** (or other similarly shaped object) to smooth out kinks in the wire.

Flexible plastic bobbins (often sold as kumihimo bobbins) are great for keeping your weaving wires tangle-free and out of the way. They are especially handy when weaving with two or more wires simultaneously.

Use a **ruler** and **fine-tip permanent marker** for measuring and marking distances on wires.

Tape is used to hold wire bundles and other design elements together during weaving. Choose the easy-release blue painter's tape or artist's tape that does not leave sticky residue when removed.

Metalworking Tools

Jeweler's hammers (forming, small ball peen) are used to flatten and texture frame wires.

A **steel bench block or** small **anvil** is used as a hammering surface for forging wire.

Use a **fine-tooth metal hand file** to even and smooth wire ends.

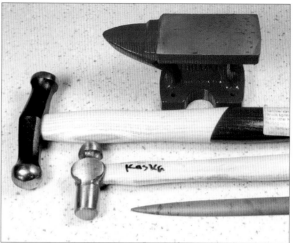

Hot Tools

Use a **butane** or **propane torch** for balling up the ends of frame wires.

Use a glass or metal **quenching bowl** for quenching the hot wire in water to cool it down.

A pair of **cross-locking tweezers** holds wire while you're heating it with a torch. It's best to use tweezers with insulated handles that will stop heat from transferring to your hand. Do not use your good tweezers for this purpose, as the heat will weaken the metal in the tool.

Wear **safety glasses** to protect your eyes when working with flame and chemicals.

Patina Tools and Supplies

Use **liver of sulfur** to patinate, or to give metal an antique look. Use either hot or cold water—hot water will speed up the process (a **mug warmer** keeps the water hot).

Place jewelry in a **rinsing bowl** after removing it from the liver of sulfur bath to stop the chemical reaction. Add baking soda to the water to help stop the reaction even faster.

Grade #0000 **steel wool** removes excess patina and adds highlights to the metal.

A **soft-bristled toothbrush** helps brush out any steel wool fibers that may lodge themselves between the weaves. Make sure you are brushing in the direction of the weaves.

Wear **rubber** or **latex gloves** to protect your hands when working with chemicals.

Finishing Tools and Supplies

A **tumbler**, along with stainless steel shot, water, and a few drops of dish soap, hardens and polishes metal.

Stainless steel mixed shot is great for polishing metal. To make sure your shot can get into all the little crevices created by the weaves, use the mixed shot that includes different shapes and sizes.

Have a **strainer** handy for rinsing steel shot between uses.

Other Useful Tools

A **ring mandrel** with a holder is an essential tool when making rings. The holder allows you to have both hands free when shaping a ring. Instead of the holder, you can use a bench vise to clamp your mandrel.

A **bench vise** is great for holding shaping tools, such as the ring and the bracelet mandrel, as well as various dowels.

A **bracelet mandrel** is used for shaping bracelets. You can also use a common round household object, such as a bottle or a drinking glass.

A **plastic** or **rawhide mallet** will not mar metal. Use it along with bracelet and ring mandrels to shape finished jewelry. You can also use it to help you form frame wires in preparation for weaving.

Use an assortment of **dowels** for shaping ear wires, frame wires, bails, and hoops.

Use two pairs of **bentnose pliers** to open and close jump rings. You can also use chainnose pliers for this task.

Choose **nylon-jaw bracelet forming pliers (right)** for forming woven bracelets.

Choose **bail-making pliers** for forming loops of an even size.

A **caliper** is helpful for figuring out sizes of beads, cabochons, and other objects.

A **wire gauge** is a great tool to have on hand to check size when you forget to label your wire or different sized wires get mixed up together.

Use a **jeweler's polishing cloth** for cleaning and smoothing out wire.

A **sketchbook** and **pencil** are helpful for recording your ideas and observations.

Wire Techniques

Wire Wrapping

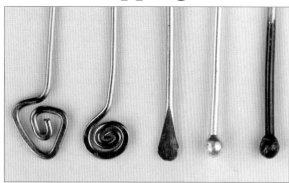

Headpins

A headpin is a short piece of wire with a stopper, or head, at one end (such as a ball or a paddle) that prevents a bead from sliding off the wire. You can purchase headpins from a jewelry supply store, or you can create your own. A simple way to make a headpin is to ball up the end of the wire with a torch (see p. 19). You can also forge the wire end to create a paddle, or twist it into a decorative spiral or other shape.

Simple bead dangle

1. String a bead on a headpin. Bend the wire above the bead at a 90° angle.
2. Using roundnose pliers, make a loop.
3. Trim the end of the wire.

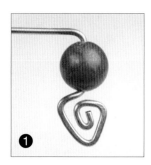
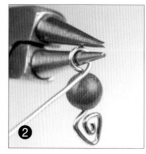

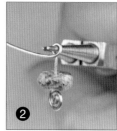

Wrapped bead dangle

1. String a bead on a headpin. Using flatnose pliers, bend the wire a little distance above the bead at a 90° angle.

NOTE:
The distance between the top of the bead and the bend will determine how many wraps you'll need.

2. Grasp the wire at the bend with roundnose pliers, and make a loop.
3. Holding the loop with flatnose pliers, wrap the end of the wire tightly and uniformly around the wire above the bead, starting at the base of the loop and wrapping down toward the bead. Trim the end of the wire when you reach the top of the bead.

Wrapped drop dangle

1. String a drop on a piece of wire. Bend both wire ends up and toward each other until they cross above the drop. Where they cross, bend one end straight up and the other at a 90° angle to the first end.
2. Wrap one wire end tightly and uniformly around the other end two or three times.
3. Make a loop with the other wire end the same way as in the wrapped bead dangle.

Bead connectors

1. Using a 2- or 3-in. section of wire, make a wrapped loop the same way as in the wrapped bead dangle. String the bead on the wire.
2. Make a wrapped loop on the other end.

Bead clusters

To create a bead cluster, simply hang several bead or drop dangles from a jump ring. To make an elongated cluster, connect two or more jump rings in a simple chain, and then attach one or more dangles to each jump ring.

Easy hook clasp

1. Ball up both ends of a 3–5-in. piece of wire (see p. 19). Grasp the wire about ¼–½ in. from one end with roundnose or bail-making pliers, and loop the end around the pliers' jaw to shape the hook. Bend the tip of the hook slightly up.

2. Shape the other end of wire into an open spiral. Use a planishing hammer to hammer the top of the hook and the spiral to harden the metal and give it a bit of texture.

NOTE:

Instead of balling up the wire ends, you can flatten the tip of the hook with a hammer or make a small loop using roundnose pliers.

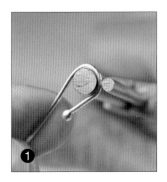
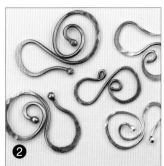

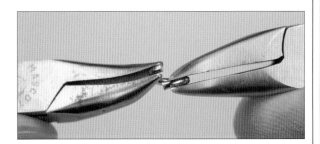

Opening and closing jump rings

Hold the jump ring with two pairs of pliers, one on either side of the split. Twist the pliers in opposite directions to open the ring sideways (as opposed to pulling the ends apart). To close the ring, twist the pliers in reverse until the ring's ends line up. Also use this method for simple bead dangles and ear wires.

Shaping Frame Wire

Hand-shaping

When it comes to shaping thicker wire, the instinct is to reach for a tool. However, some of my most successful large-gauge wire bending is done by hands alone. Hand shaping gives your wire a more organic look. When using your hands, you can feel the wire's energy as it expands and contracts with each bend. You are able to gauge how far you can push it before it gets too stiff to manipulate any further. And your hands will not nick the wire.

Try these exercises:

Cut a few 5-in. pieces of 18-gauge copper wire. Smooth them out so they are all bump-free.

1. Holding the ends of one of the wires with your fingers, slowly bring your hands toward each other, making the wire bend in the middle. See how far you can go without creating sharp a peak. Now, without repositioning your fingers, move your hands in and out, up and down, and sideways to see what the wire will do for you and how fast it will start to work-harden.

2. Pick up another wire. Start by making a bend in the middle the way you did in the first exercise.

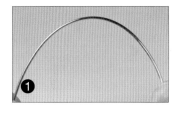

Keep bending the wire until the ends cross and it forms a loop. Pull on the ends of the wire to tighten the loop. After the loop gets small, reverse direction to bring your hands closer together and make the loop bigger. Try adjusting the size and shape of the loop by just pushing and pulling the wire ends.

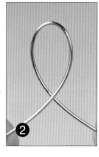

3. Pick up another wire. Use different parts of your fingers as shaping mandrels to make soft, freeform waves.

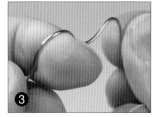

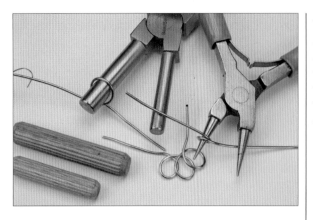

Shaping with tools

For **circular loops**, use dowels, roundnose pliers, and other tools that will match the shape you want to create.

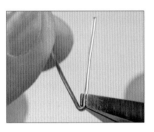 

To make **pointed bends** in the frame wire, use one jaw of your flatnose pliers as the bending edge. For sharp angles, use the tips of the pliers For 90° angles, bend the wire against the wider part of the jaw, toward the back of the pliers.

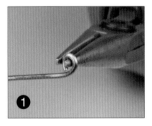 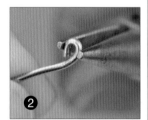

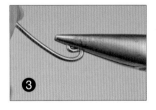 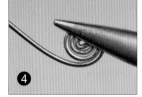

To create a **tight spiral**:
1. Make a small loop at the end of the wire with the tips of the chainnose pliers.
2. Squeeze the loop with the pliers to make it smaller.
3. Hold the loop in the pliers' jaws, and spiral the wire around the center.
4. Reposition the pliers as the spiral grows.

To create an **open spiral**, make a loop at the end of the wire the same way as when forming the tight spiral. Without repositioning the pliers, grasp the other end of the wire with your fingers and loosely spiral the wire around the center.

Filing

Use a fine-tooth file to smooth out wire ends that will not be balled up.
1. Hold the file at a 90° angle to the end of the wire. File in one direction away from yourself.
2. To file the wire at an angle, hold the file at the desired angle to the end of the wire, and start by filing at one corner. Continue filing until the entire surface of the end is one plane.

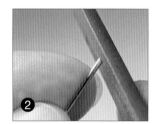

Forging

Forging (or hammering) refers to using a hammer to flatten, expand, and texture metal. Forging also work-hardens the metal and makes it stronger.

Forging with the flatter side of the hammer will produce a smooth finish, and hammering with the more rounded side will result in a textured finish. The rounder and smaller the peen, the smaller and deeper the dimples left on the metal will be.

Forge to texture and strengthen wire spirals, hook clasps, and ear wires, as well as to create paddle ends on headpins. Make sure not to hammer the metal too thin, or it will become brittle.

Balling Up Wire

CAUTION:

Don't attempt to heat wires that have color coating applied to them. The different finishes contain chemicals that release toxic fumes when burned.

Work above a fireproof surface, such as a soldering pad or ceramic tile. Make sure that your torch's nozzle is pointing away from anything flammable, including you and other people, and then light the torch. Grip the wire with cross-locking tweezers, and place the end of it in the hottest part of the flame. If you want the ball to be round, hold the wire straight up and down, perpendicular to the tabletop. Holding it at an angle will allow gravity to pull the melting metal off-center, making the ball skew to one side. When the end of the wire begins to melt, the melted metal will start to form a ball. As the ball gets larger, it will move up the wire, consuming the metal above it. Follow the ball with the torch, making sure the hottest part of the flame is always on the ball. If you move the flame too high, the wire above the ball will melt, and the ball will break off and fall. Remove the wire from the flame when the ball reaches the desired size **(photo 1)**.

CAUTION:

The entire wire, not just the ball, as well as the tweezers and the nozzle of the torch will be extremely hot. Allow sufficient cool-down time before handling the wire or the tools.

To cool the wire, either quench it in a bowl of water for instant cool-down, or set it on a heat-resistant surface and let it air-cool slowly. Fast cool-down will produce different colors than slow cool-down. For example, sterling silver will turn dark gray if air-cooled and light gray when quenched in water instantly after being heated. Copper will turn dark, almost black, when air cooled and turn reddish when quenched in water. You can remove some of the color with steel wool.

When balling up the end of a wire that has already been woven into a design, you have to be careful not to bring the flame too close to the finished jewelry, especially if it contains stones or beads. Bend the wire in such a way that its end is as far away from the rest of the piece as possible and pointing down, and then bring the wire end into the torch flame **(photo 2)**.

When the wire to be balled up is very short and exiting the middle of the piece, hold the jewelry parallel to the tabletop with the wire perpendicular to it and pointing down. Hold the flame below and parallel to the jewelry piece as you ball up the wire **(photo 3)**.

NOTE:

For most people, it is fun and easy to learn to ball up the wires. However, if you prefer not to use the torch, you don't have to. You can simply make small spirals at the wire ends.

Sterling silver (left), copper (middle), fine silver (right).

Weaving

Making your weave smooth and even

Smooth out the frame wires: Straighten and smooth out all the frame wires before starting your project and take care not to twist them up while shaping your piece and during the weaving process. Make sure that the wires that are supposed to be straight are perfectly straight, and the wires that are supposed to be curved or looped have a smooth and bump-free arc. Keep in mind that any bumps and kinks on the frame wire will ultimately show up in your weave and become part of your design, whether you planned it that way or not.

Maintain proper spacing between frame wires: Always leave enough space between frame wires for the weaving wire to pass through. In parallel weaves, that space should be even throughout the length of the weave. The thicker the weaving wire, the wider the space between the frame wires needs to be. It is also important to keep the correct spacing between frame wires that are not parallel, such as in silhouettes, where the shapes can easy be distorted if correct distance is not kept between the wires.

I find that the best way to maintain desired spacing is to avoid pulling on the weaving wire as you bring it across to create a weave **(photo 1)**. Pulling it across will push the frame wires together, making it difficult to control the spacing between them. Instead, always pull the weaving wire at a 90° angle to the weave as you tighten the loop around the frame wires **(photo 2)**.

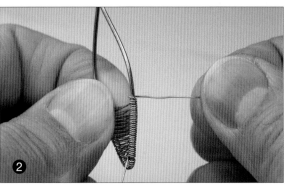

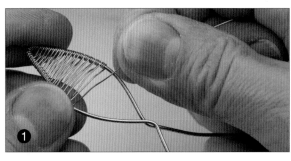

Correct

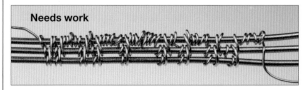

Needs work

Maintain even tension on the weaving wire:
• Pull the weaving wire tight against frame wires with each wraparound.
• Make sure the wire is straight and flat as you draw it over or between frame wires.
• Keep uniform spacing between individual weaves.

Preventing and removing kinks

It is important to keep the wire as kink-free as possible and to remove any kinks that do occur right away. Here are several tips that will help you keep your work kink-free:

Work from the spool: Whenever you can, it is best to work from-the-spool. That means leaving your weaving wire rolled up on the spool it came on and unrolling a little at the time—only as much as you are comfortable working with. Having only a short section of wire free from the spool will help with the kinking-up problem. Also, when the wire is left on the spool, you don't have to worry about how much of it you will need to cut off to have enough to complete a particular section. Simply weave until you are finished, and then snip it off. No underestimating or overestimating, no waste.

If the original spool is too bulky and gets in your way, measure and cut the length of the weaving wire you need, and then wind it onto a lighter, smaller, flexible plastic spool.

Do not allow the weaving wire to twist and loop: Make sure the weaving wire maintains a gentle curve throughout its length. Straighten it out as soon as you notice it starting to twist or cross itself.

Take extra care when threading the weaving wire: The weaving wire tends to kink most when it is being threaded or pulled through tight spots, such as in the netting technique, when stitching, and when working on a part of a design where the frame wires create a closed loop. To stop weaving wires from twisting, place a pen or similar object (I often use my finger) inside the loop created by the weaving wire and let the wire glide over it **(photo 3)**. As you continue pulling and the loop gets smaller, replace the pen

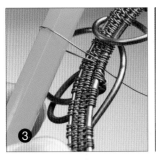

with something much thinner, such as the tip of your needle tool, and then tighten the loop around it **(photo 4)**. Next, remove the needle tool and pull the wire all the way through.

Un-knot the kink as soon as it occurs: Don't run your fingers down the wire as you might with a thread. That will only tighten the kink and make it impossible to unravel. Instead, hold the wire with your fingers on either side of the kink **(photo 5)** and push the wires toward the middle, forcing the loop to enlarge **(photo 6)**. Uncross the ends and smooth out the wire.

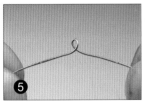

Smooth out the wire: Any time the wire gets crunched up, make sure to smooth it out before resuming weaving. Hold a pencil (or some other dowel-like object) in your fist with your thumb pressed tightly against its shank. Place the wire under your thumb and pull the section of wire that needs to be straightened across the dowel. Repeat several times until the wire is smooth.

Fixing mistakes

When weaving, it is very easy to miscount and accidently skip a weave or add an extra wrap. As you work, it's a good idea to check your weave frequently. (Make sure you also look at the back; sometimes a mistake is much easier to spot that way.) When something doesn't look right, it probably isn't, even if you can't tell right away what went wrong. Examine the weave under a magnifying glass to help figure it out. When you pinpoint where the trouble started, undo the section of the weave up to and including the mistake. Smooth out the unwrapped section of the wire (see above). Resume weaving, keeping in mind that the length of wire that you just unwrapped is weakened and needs to be treated gently.

Adding a new weaving wire

You will need to start a new weaving wire every time you run out of wire before finishing a weave or when your wire breaks. Depending on the weave pattern and where the break occurs, adding wire can be very noticeable or hardly visible at all. When you know that the piece of wire you are working with is about to run out, you can plan to finish it off in a place where the fix can be easier to blend in. When your wire snaps unexpectedly, you may want to undo a portion of your weave to reach that place. Sometimes the point of the break is in a spot where there just no way to hide the mend without undoing a lot of weaving. In such a case, you may want to just fix it the best you can and let it go.

Adding wire in a coil: One of the best places to add a new wire is along a coiled section of the weave. Trim the old weaving wire and push its end flush against the frame wire. Then, start a new weaving wire where the old one ends. Make sure the new wire runs in the same direction as the old one and the two cut ends fit snugly together. Try to hide the seam in the back.

Adding wire in over-under weave: Over-under weave is the hardest to hide a mend in, especially when there is a wide stretch of weave between frame wires, such as in a crescent or a leaf shape. If you want your weave to be perfect, you may have to undo the section of the weave to where the shape you are working on began and redo it completely. Otherwise, simply wrap the old wire end a couple of times around one of the frame wires and trim. Start the new weaving wire by wrapping it two or three times around the frame wire on the opposite side. Make sure the new wire runs in the same direction as the old one.

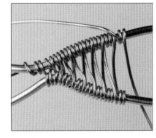

Adding wire in over-over weave: Over-over weave is very similar to over-under weave. Undo and redo the weave if possible. Otherwise, patch it up the same way you would the over-under weave.

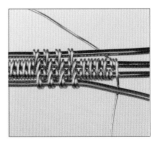

Adding wire in looping: In looping, you are working with short sections of wires, so you will finish them off and start new ones frequently. Wrap the end of the old wire around the loop just above the one you are working on a few times **(photo 1)**. Trim. Start a new wire by wrapping it around the wire of the last loop a couple of times **(photo 2)**.

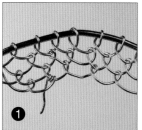 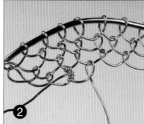

Finishing off tail ends of weaving wire

I leave most of the weaving wire ends uncut until I am done weaving. I like to use short sections of weaving wire to fasten a bead or stitch a wire curlicue, and it's much easier to use a wire that is already attached than to start a new one. When I am finished, I go around and remove or tuck in all the ends using one of the following methods:

1. Break it: When the end wire is coming up from between a tightly woven section, it's best to trim it at its base: Hold the end of the wire between your thumb and index finger and, keeping it taut, move it back and forth until it breaks.

2. Trim the wire close to the frame wire with wire cutters: Make sure the trimmed end is in a location that will not catch on something and unravel.

3. In areas where it looks like the wire may come undone if not secured, you can wrap the end of it around another section of the weaving wire and then trim it.

Stitching

Stitching is a finishing technique used in freeform weaving for securing loose parts and for attaching beads, wire curlicues, and other embellishments. Stitching is usually done after the main weaving phase of the project is finished. Beads attached with stitching are added on top of the woven section, or fastened to the parts of frame wires not covered by the weaves.

NOTE:
The techniques for incorporating beads into the weaves will be covered in "The Weaves" chapter.

Stitching with wire is very much like stitching with thread, minus the needle. Think of it as sewing on a button—in-and-out, in-and-out. There are very few rules when it comes to stitching. Each situation requires a different approach, and many times you will just have to figure it out as you go along. The goal is to make the stitches blend in with the weave and become part of the design.

Stitching on wire ends

To keep your stitches looking orderly, follow these simple guidelines when possible:
• Depending on the weave type, go across only one or two frame wires at a time.
• Run the stitching wire between the weaves, not on top of them.
• Do not let stitches cross the weaves or one another.
• Run stitches in the same directions as the weave.
• Use the same gauge wire as the one used for weaving.

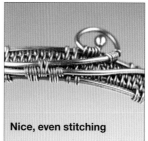 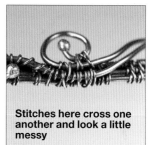

Nice, even stitching

Stitches here cross one another and look a little messy

Stitching on beads

Method #1: To stitch one bead on top of a woven section:
1. String a bead in the center of a 3–4-in. piece of weaving wire. Bend the wire on either side of the bead straight down. Thread the bent ends of the wire through the spaces between the weaves on either side of the spot where you want the bead to rest.
2. Bring the wires back to the front, threading them through the spaces between the weaves adjacent to the ones you used for the first thread.

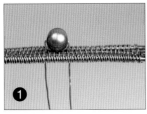

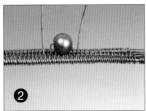

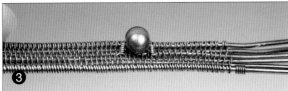

3. To secure the bead, tightly wrap the ends of the wire several times around the wires on either side of the bead.

Method #2: To stitch a row or a cluster of beads on the surface of a woven section:

1. Follow steps 1 and 2 in Method #1, except use a longer piece of wire (the length depends on how many beads you're adding) and string the first bead on the wire toward one end. When you bend the wire down, you will end up with one short and one long end. Thread the wire ends down and up.

2. Secure the shorter wire in place by wrapping it around the wire on the side of the bead a few times. Slide a second bead onto the longer end of the wire, and thread the wire down and up again. Add as many beads as you like in a line or a cluster. Finish by wrapping the end of the wire around the wire on the side of the last bead several times.

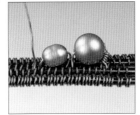

Method #3: To stitch beads in the bend of a frame wire or inside a loop:

1. String a bead to the center of a 3–4-in. piece of weaving wire. Holding the bead in the bend of the frame, wire-wrap

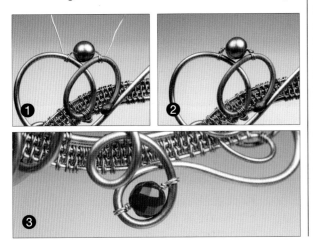

the two ends of the weaving wire once or twice around the frame wire on either side of the bead.

2. Wrap the ends around the weaving wire on either side of the bead.

3. Wrap a bead inside a loop using this method as well.

Using a needle tool to make spaces between weaves

You will often have to enlarge a space between weaves to make an opening large enough for weaving wire to pass through. The best way to do this is with a needle tool. Place the tip of the needle between the weaves where you want the opening to be, and then wiggle the tool back and forth as you push the needle into and through the weave. Be sure that your fingers are out of the way

when the needle's point pokes through on the back. When the weave is very tight, making it hard to get the needle in, you can get more leverage if you place the piece flat on top of a piece of scrap wood and bring the needle tool down, through the weave; let the tip go into the wood.

Finishing

Adding patina with liver of sulfur

All metals react with the environment and change their appearance as they are exposed to oxygen and other elements. Silver, copper and bronze jewelry, if left exposed, will oxidize over time and develop a rich, dark patina that adds contrast and dimension to the details and makes the jewelry look vintage or antique. You can create the look of oxidizing by dipping your jewelry in a **liver of sulfur (LOS) solution**.

LOS is a chemical that is used to add patina to metals. It comes in liquid, gel, and rock form. Each formula has its advantages and disadvantages. Gel and liquid are very convenient to use; just pour a little into a cup of hot water, and you are ready to go. Gel form is very stable and will not degrade over time, even when left uncapped. Once dissolved in water, though, it neutralizes very quickly and becomes ineffective. The liquid concentrate will last longer when diluted, and it can be reused over a period of several days. It will degrade over time, though, even in its concentrated state. The rock form is the least expensive; however, it also deteriorates when exposed to air and moisture.

LOS is safe to use with most stones. It can stain some materials other than metal, but so far I have not had that happen to anything I worked with in this book.

I use mostly the rock form of LOS, but gel works, too. LOS solution made out of rock form can be saved and reheated over a period of two to four days. Active solution will be yellow-green in color and have a sulfur (rotten egg) smell to it. When it becomes milky white and loses most of the odor, it is no longer effective. To dispose of used LOS, mix it with some baking soda to make sure it is completely neutralized, dilute it with water, and then pour it down the drain.

Place a pea-sized chunk of rock LOS in a cup of hot (not boiling) water. Mix until the rock dissolves completely. (Or make a solution according to the manufacturer's instructions.)

Wash the piece you want to add patina to with soap and water to remove any residue (such as oily fingerprints) that may prevent it from oxidizing evenly. You can dip the jewelry in hot water to warm it up prior to placing it in LOS to speed up oxidation **(photo 1)**. Submerge the entire piece in the LOS solution.

Cover the cup to cut down on fumes, if desired, and watch through the glass as the piece darkens **(photo 2)**. It will take a few seconds or several minutes to patinate your piece, depending on how strong and how warm the solution is— as well as the type of metal in your jewelry. Remove the from the LOS when all the metal turns evenly dark gray. Rinse well, and dry.

Brush the oxidized metal with #0000 grade steel wool to remove patina from the raised areas and bring out the highlights.

Three stages: prior to being dipped (left), evenly oxidized (center), and highlighted with steel wool (right)

Tumble-finishing

A tumbler cleans, polishes, and works-hardens metals. There are rotating, vibrating, and magnetic tumblers. I use a rotating tumbler. A rotating tumbler consists of two main parts: a plastic or a rubber drum with a watertight lid and a base with two rollers that the drum sits on top of. The rollers are powered by a small motor that makes them rotate, which in turn turns the drum. When the jewelry and stainless steel shot tumble together inside the drum, the mirror-smooth shot burnishes the metal's surfaces by repeatedly brushing against them.

All solid, uncoated, and gold- and silver-filled wires can be tumbled for several hours or longer. Pieces that are made with wire alone, especially ones made with dead-soft wire, will only benefit from prolonged tumbling. When tumbling jewelry containing stones and beads, you have to be more careful. Agates, jaspers, carnelian, quartz crystal and other hard stones, as well as most good-quality glass, do well in the tumbler. However some softer stones, such as malachite or turquoise, can be dulled by the tumbling process and many lower-quality beads have surface coatings that can get scratched off.

Test to see if the stones or beads you intend to use will withstand the tumbling process: Place several beads and/or stones in the tumbler. Tumble for 15 minutes, and then check to see if the beads or stones are damaged. If they seem to be OK, tumble for another 15 minutes and check again. Repeat a few more times. Checking every so often will let you know how long it is safe to tumble them.

Do not tumble porous organic materials, such as wood, feathers, soft bone, or coral.

1. Place the stainless steel shot in the drum, and then fill it with water to about ½–1 in. above the shot. Add a few drops of dishwashing liquid. Place the jewelry in the tumbler, replace the lid and turn it on. You can tumble more than one piece at a time, but try not to overcrowd.
2. When finished tumbling, remove the jewelry from the drum, rinse it well under running water, and dry.

Use a drain basket to catch any shot that might fall into the sink during rinsing.

3. To clean the tumbler, pour the stainless steel shot into a strainer and rinse it. Rinse the drum. Place the shot back into the drum, loosely cover with the lid, and set aside for the next tumbling session.

Chapter 1
The Weaves

This chapter covers five weaving techniques needed to complete all the projects in this book: over-under weave, over-over weave, coiling, looping, and circular weaving (which is a variation of the first two). It is likely that you will recognize the techniques shown here from everyday objects around you, and perhaps also from having worked with some of them yourself in different applications. For example, the over-under weave is universally used for basket-making, as well as in loom-weaving fabrics, tapestries, and rugs. Looping is a sewing technique often employed in hemming garments and in decorative stitching, such as embroidery. It has also been used for centuries by Native Americans to craft beautiful dream catchers. Coiling is used in making braided rag rugs, often associated with country-style décor, as well as in creating exquisite pine-needle and fabric baskets.

Each of the five techniques presented here is covered in a separate section that includes a description and explanation of the technique, as well as two or more projects that demonstrate the practical design applications of that technique.

I encourage you to start at the beginning of the chapter and work your way through it in order. The complexity of the projects increases as you go, and you may also need to know one or more techniques from the previous instructions or weaves to complete a project later on.

Learn to use circular weaving, as shown here, to create a beautiful beaded pendant.

Over-Under Weave (Basket Weave)

Let's start our venture into the world of weaving with the over-under weave that most of us are already familiar with. We come in contact with it every day, in fabrics, baskets, rugs, and other common objects. Most people associate weaving in general with this type of weave.

The simplest pattern of over-under weave, called *plaiting* in basket-making, is created when strips of material (wire in this case) wind in and out (or over and under) between similar strands arranged parallel to each other and at a 90° angle to the first set of strips **(figure 1)**. The resulting crisscrossing grid holds all the wires together, transforming a collection of individual strands into a usable component that, in jewelry-making, can become a body of a bracelet, a bail for a pendant, or a bezel for a cabochon.

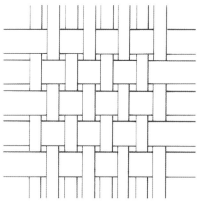

figure 1

techniques

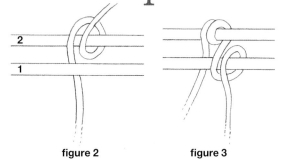

figure 2   figure 3

figure 4

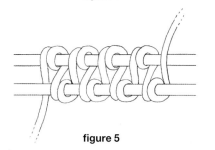

figure 5

Basic double over-under weave

Begin a basic double over-under weave with two frame wires that run parallel to each other. The space between them should be equal to at least double the thickness of the weaving wire.

To start the over-under weave, focus on the path of the weaving wire. The weaving wire first travels under frame wire 1 and then over frame wire 2, making a loop around frame wire 2 **(figure 2)**. After the loop is pulled tight against frame wire 2, the weaving wire makes a U-turn. It travels under frame wire 2 and over frame wire 1, and loops around frame wire 1 **(figure 3)**. Next, it makes a U-turn to go under frame wire 1 and over frame wire 2 **(figure 4)**. This pattern repeats as the weaving wire travels back and forth—under, over, and around—the frame wires **(figure 5)**.

Basic three-wire over-under weave

If you were successful with the double weave described above, this variation of over-under weave should give you no trouble. As you probably guessed, the three-wire weave is created using three frame wires (numbered 1, 2, and 3 in figures 6–9) that run parallel to one another with spaces between each pair equal to at least double the thickness of the weaving wire.

As in the double weave, in a three-wire weave, the weaving wire first travels under frame wire 1 and then over frame wire 2. However, instead of making a U-turn at this point, it continues up to travel under and to loop around frame wire 3 **(figure 6)**. After the loop is pulled tight against frame wire 3, the weaving wire makes a U-turn. On its return, it goes over frame wire 3, under frame wire 2, over and around frame wire 1 **(figure 7)**, and makes a U-turn **(figure 8)**. Then it repeats the pattern until desired length is reached **(figure 9)**.

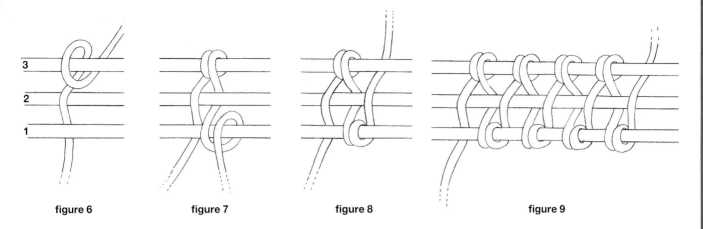

3

2

1

figure 6   figure 7   figure 8   figure 9

Four- and more wire weave

The technique for weaving with four, five, or more frame wires is pretty much the same as weaving with three wires. The weaving wire should follow the over-and-under pattern across all the frame wires, no matter the number, making sure that with each weave across, the weaving wire goes over the frame wires that it was previously under and under the wires that it was previously over. At the end of each pass-through (both up and down), the weaving wire needs to wrap completely around the last frame wire and make a U-turn to start the next weave (photo a).

Wrap-arounds

Instructions in other books or tutorials may require you to return the weaving wire at the last frame wire with just a simple turn. It is a valid technique; however, I prefer to do the complete wrap-around, which locks the border frame wires into place and prevents them from shifting out of position. The simple turn-around results in a much less uniform weave (photo b).

Varying the compactness of the weaves

One easy way to add more texture and contrast to your weaving is to vary the compactness of your weaves. To do this, you simply need to add extra wraps (or coils) between the weaves at each U-turn. The additional wraps will push the wires farther apart, making the weave less dense and more airy-looking. The more coils you add, the more open the weave will become (photo c).

The instructions for some projects in this book specify the number of coils to use. To get the right number, you will have to add an extra wrap to the number of coils the instructions call for. For example, if you need to have two coils between each weave, you will wrap three times: once for the weave itself, and twice for the coils between.

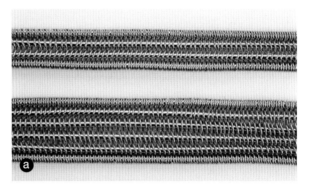

Four-wire weave (top) and six-wire weave (bottom).

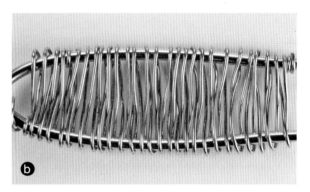

With the simple turn-around, it is very difficult to control the spacing of both the frame and the weaving wires.

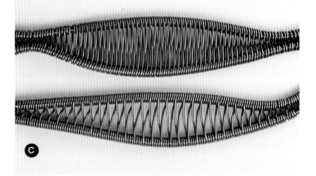

The top weave was woven with one wrap between each weave; the bottom weave has three wraps.

Woven ribbons

Ribbons are two or more frame wires woven together into long strips. Ribbons woven with over-under weave, as well as those created with the over-over weaving technique described in the next section, can be used for making cuff bracelets, ring bands, bezels for stones, and for braiding. Personally, I prefer to use over-over weave ribbon for most of these situations, reserving over-under weave for designs requiring the use of the two-dimensional shapes I call silhouettes (see below). Having said that, I do think that bracelets made with over-under weave ribbons, especially the wavy and non-parallel versions **(photos d, e)**, are absolutely beautiful. Also, some bezels work better when made with over-under technique.

Parallel ribbons are woven using sets of frame wires arranged side by side and running parallel to each other (or in flat bundles) as described in basic over-under weave.

Freeform ribbons are woven with non-parallel frame wires and resemble a string of leaf-like shapes. As they are being woven, they should be treated like leaf silhouettes (see p. 29). For example, when a segment of the ribbon looks like an asymmetrical leaf, add extra wraps between weaves on the side of the larger bump. Note that the ribbon's weaving pattern is based solely on the shapes of the outside wires and therefore the frame wires that are in the middle of the ribbon can be shaped independently of the outside wires.

Wave ribbons are not the same as parallel ribbons that have been woven and then shaped into waves. In the wave ribbons, the frame wires are shaped prior to being woven, forming a string of narrow crescent shapes that have to be woven just like the crescent silhouettes (see below). It means that, in order to fill in the gaps between the weaves you need to add extra wraps of weaving wire to the outside (larger) curve of every wave. Doing this will result in tightly coiled edges that look nice and uniform and also have a practical advantage of preventing the ribbon from straightening out when tugged.

Silhouettes

A silhouette is created when the space between two frame wires widens to form a two-dimensional shape that is then filled in with a weave spanning the distance between the two frame wires. The over-under weave is uniquely suited for building silhouettes because of its crisscrossing pattern, which adds beauty and strength to the weaves.

The silhouette shapes are often designed to be separate components, to be used individually as charms, earrings, or pendants, or strung together to form necklaces or bracelets. Silhouettes can also be used within, and be an integral part of, more complex designs. For example, in the Winged Pendant, p. 99, the leaf silhouette is shaped to become a bail, and crescent shapes become the wings.

The silhouettes are a little more challenging to weave than basic parallel weaves because the frame wires outlining them are angled. When weaving from the wide end toward the narrow end, you'll find the weaves tend to slide down the sloping sides, creating gaps between them. Because the length of each individual weave is different than all the others, there is no way to push the weaves back together when they spread apart, as you would in the parallel weave. When weaving the wedge silhouette, you can avoid this problem by simply weaving from the narrow to the open end. In the shapes that are tapered on both ends (crescent and both versions of the leaf), you must also weave down to the narrow end when working on the second half of the shape. When weaving down, push the section of the weave that has already been formed up and hold it in place each time you create a new weave. This can be difficult, and the only way to get good at it is through practice. When working on your own designs, remember that elongated and relatively narrow shapes are easier to weave than ones that are short and fat.

Identifying the shapes in your designs will help you to use proper weaving techniques, resulting in neater, tighter weaves.

A **crescent silhouette** is created when two frame wires, each shaped into an arc, one larger and one smaller, curve in the same direction with the smaller one nesting inside the

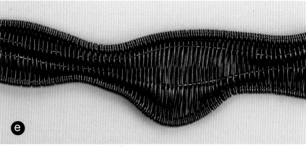

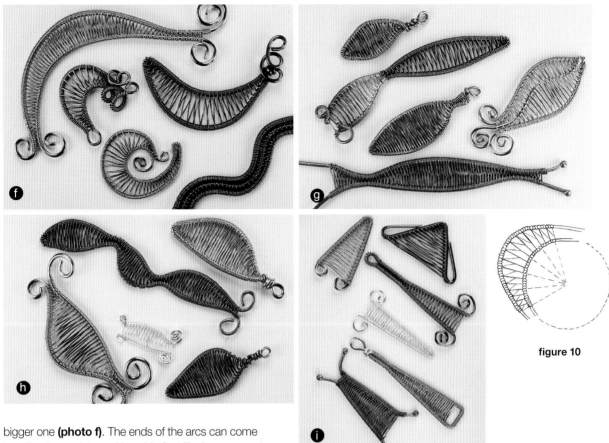

figure 10

bigger one **(photo f)**. The ends of the arcs can come together to a point on either side (just like in a crescent moon), come together on one end and remain open on the other end, or remain open on both ends.

When weaving a crescent silhouette, imagine it as a section of a circle (or a bicycle wheel) with each wire in the weave angled toward the center **(figure 10)**. To achieve this "spokes in a wheel" effect, gradually increase the number of wraps between each weave at the larger arc as you weave toward the top of the curve, and gradually decrease them as you weave down. The number of wraps you add will depend on the shape of the curve, the difference in size of (or the distance between) the two arcs, and the steepness of the curve. The bigger the difference in size, the more wraps you will have to add; the steeper the curve, the faster you will have to increase the number of wraps. Because it is often hard to figure out the angle of the wires while in the process of weaving, it is a good idea to make a drawing of your crescent shape with the weaves sketched in at their correct angles, and use the drawing as a template to follow while you weave.

A **leaf silhouette** is a symmetrical shape formed when two frame wires shaped into identical arcs curve away from each other in a mirror-image fashion **(photo g)**. Just like in the crescent shape, the two arcs forming the leaf can come to a point on each end, come together on one

end and remain open on the other, or remain open on both ends. The weave in the leaf runs perpendicular to the center line.

An **asymmetrical leaf silhouette** is the shape of a leaf with two sides that are different **(photo h)**. Because the curve of the frame wire is larger on one side than the other, you will need to add extra wraps between the weaves on the larger side in order to keep the weaves from becoming skewed or forming gaps between them. This is similar to the crescent shape, except here the goal is to keep the weaves running straight up and down, perpendicular to the center line, not at an angle.

A **wedge silhouette** is shaped like a slice of a pie **(photo i)**. Its outline is created when a section of the frame wire is bent in half, forming two sides of the wedge, or when two separate frame wires form a V. The wedge silhouette can be long and narrow, short and fat, or anything in between. The weaves in the wedge run straight across, perpendicular to the center line of the shape. To avoid weaves sliding out of place, it is best to weave the wedge from the narrow to the wide end.

Dagger
earrings

This project demonstrates how silhouette shapes, in this case a wedge, can be used as standalone components to create very simple yet intricate-looking earrings. If desired, add a simple bead dangle to complete the earrings.

tools

- Weaving tools
- Metalworking tools
- Finishing tools and supplies
- Patina tools and supplies (optional)

materials

- 8 in. 20-gauge half-hard wire
- 6 ft. 28-gauge dead-soft wire
- 14 24-gauge ⅛-in. jump rings
- Pair of ear wires
- 2 simple bead dangles (optional)

1 Cut the 20-gauge wire into two 4-in. pieces. Mark the centerpoint and then ¾ in. from both ends of each 4-in. wire.

2 Using roundnose pliers, bend each wire in the middle to form a V with ⅜-in. distance between the wire ends at the top of the V **(photo a)**.

NOTE:

You want to end up with a ¼-in. space when you're finished weaving. Since the distance between the frame wires tends to narrow during the weaving process, start with a slightly wider gap.

---

3 Cut 3 ft. of 28-gauge wire (or work off a spool). Start the weave by wrapping the weaving wire seven or eight times at the bend of a V, distributing the wraps evenly between the two sides **(photo b)**.

4 Continuing with the same wire, weave toward the open end of the wedge using the over-under weaving technique with two wraps between each weave. Keep weaving until you reach the ¾-in. marks on the frame wires. Wrap the weaving wire around one frame wire a couple of times and trim the end. Trim the tail at the start of the weave **(photo c)**.

5 File the ¾-in.-long ends of the frame wire to remove any sharp edges, and then use them to create decorative spirals **(photo d)**. At this point, you can hammer the spirals slightly to flatten and add a little texture (optional).

Skills to review:
simple bead dangle, p. 16 (optional), open spiral, p. 18, forging, p. 18, shaping frame wire, p. 18, double over-under weave, p. 26, wedge silhouette, p. 29

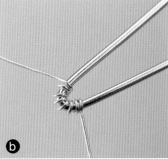

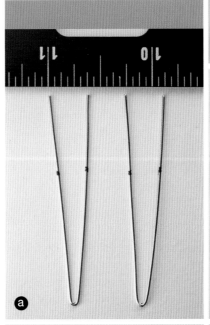

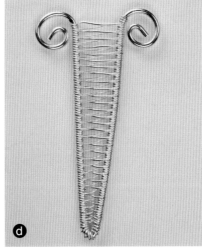

6 Make two three-link chains using six jump rings, and attach them to each spiral. Connect the two chains with another jump ring **(photo e)**. Attach an ear wire to the center jump ring. Add simple bead dangles to the bottom of each earring, if desired.

7 Repeat steps 3–6 to make a second earring.

8 Apply liver of sulfur solution (optional). Tumble for 20 minutes.

Freeform
toggle clasp

In the previous project, you discovered how silhouettes can be used as individual elements to create simple designs. Here, you will start to link and combine these elements to generate slightly more complicated forms. As you work on this piece, notice how the eye part of the clasp is made of a crescent shape formed into a circle, and the toggle bar consists of two wedge shapes joined in the center.

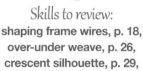

Make the eye

1 Cut an 8-in. and a 5-in. piece of 18-gauge wire. Measure and mark the 8-in. frame wire 4½ in. from one end. Grasp the wire at the mark with roundnose pliers, where the jaw measures approximately ⅛ in., and loop both wire ends around one jaw until they cross one another and make a complete circle **(photo a)**.

2 Mark both wires where they intersect. Grip one of the wires with flatnose pliers slightly above the mark, and bend it outward. Repeat with the other wire. They should now run in the same direction with a narrow space (about ¹⁄₁₆ in.) below the loop **(photo b)**.

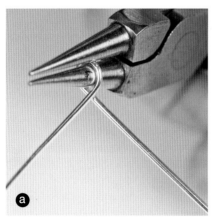

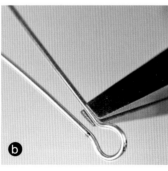

Skills to review:
**shaping frame wires, p. 18,
over-under weave, p. 26,
crescent silhouette, p. 29,
wedge silhouette, p. 29**

Tools
- Weaving tools
- Finishing tools and supplies
- Patina tools and supplies (optional)

Materials
- 13 in. 18-gauge half-hard wire
- 12 ft. 28-gauge dead-soft wire
- 3–4mm round bead (optional)

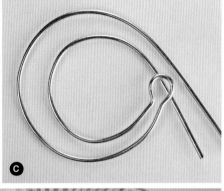

(c)

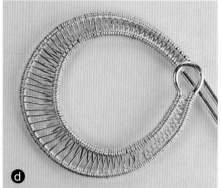

(d)

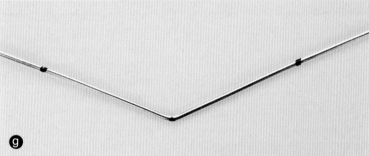

(e)

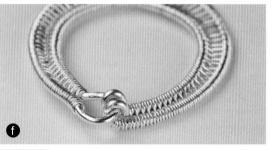

(f)

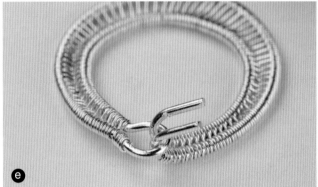

(g)

template 1

3 Shape the clasp's eye using **template 1**. Make sure that the longer wire forms the outer edge of the circle **(photo c)**.

4 Working off the spool, start weaving at the base of the loop you made in step 1. Continue weaving up and all the way around the eye. Don't forget to gradually increase and then decrease the number of wraps between the weaves on the outside wire as you go up and down the arc of the eye. Lay your piece on top of the template from time to time to check for accuracy. Readjust the frame wires as necessary. When you reach the end of the circle, wrap the weaving wire a couple of times around one of the frame

wires and trim the end. Also trim the tail at the start of the weave **(photo d)**.

5 Cut each end of the frame wires to ¼ in. beyond the end of the weave. Line them up with the loop, and then bend them up and thread them through the loop **(photo e)**. Use roundnose pliers to bend the ends down until they touch the woven section and capture the loop. Trim the wires as necessary to make a tight fit **(photo f)**.

Make the bar

6 Mark the centerpoint of the 5-in. 18-gauge wire. Mark ⅞ in. on either side of the center. Bend the wire at the centerpoint to match the angle in the template **(template 2 and photo g)**.

7 With roundnose pliers (where the jaw measures about ⅛ in. across), grasp the wire at one of the ¾-in. marks. Bend the wire around the pliers' jaw until it meets the center mark **(photo h)**.

8 Mark the wire where it touches the center, and then place the jaw of the flatnose pliers at the mark and bend the wire down.

9 Repeat step 7 to shape the other arm. Do not bend this wire **(photo i)**.

10 Wrap the straight end of the frame wire around the bent end two times, and then cut it off. Trim the remaining wire end to ¼ in. Make a loop using roundnose pliers **(photo j)**.

11 Cut a 24-in. piece of the 28-gauge wire. Start in the middle of the bar and, using the double over-under weaving technique with two wraps between each weave, weave toward the end of one of the bar's arms. Note that you will have to thread the weaving wire through the loop created by the arm (see Preventing and Removing Kinks, p. 20). Weave to where the frame wire starts to bend to form the rounded end **(photo k)**. Wrap the weaving wire all the way around the curve, and then trim the end **(photo l)**.

12 Repeat step 11 for the other arm of the bar. Trim the wire tails at the center of the bar.

13 Use your fingers to shape the bar to resemble wings **(photo m)**.

14 Attach a bead in the middle of the bar to match a necklace or bracelet (optional).

Finish

15 Apply liver of sulfur solution (optional). Tumble for 20 minutes.

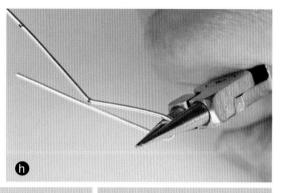

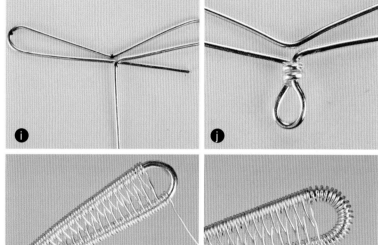

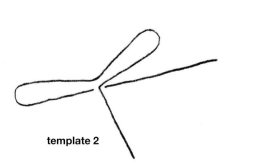

template 2

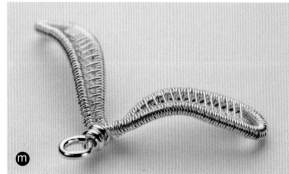

Wave
bracelet

Skills to review:
shaping frame wires: hand shaping, p. 17, forging (optional), p. 18, three-wire over-under weave, p. 26, wave ribbon, p. 28

So far, you have worked with shapes created with only two frame wires, and the weaves ran without interruption between the frame wires. This bracelet design adds a new layer of complexity by inserting an extra frame wire in the middle—so the weaving wire now goes over and under three wires instead of just two. The weave in this bracelet is continuous and varies little from beginning to end, giving you lots of practice in tension control and uniformity.

Tools
- Weaving tools
- Finishing tools and supplies
- Bracelet mandrel
- Patina tools and supplies (optional)

Materials
- 30 in. 16-gauge wire
- 15–20 ft. 26-gauge wire

NOTE:
It's best to shape each wire separately. First, shape the bottom wire and then bend the middle wire and the top wire to follow the curve of the first wire.

Make the wave

1 Cut the 16-gauge wire into one 20-in. and one 10-in. piece. Mark the center of the 20-in. wire, and then, using the roundnose pliers (where the jaw measures 3/32 in.), bend the wire in half to create a U bend. Mark both wires 1/4 in. from the bottom of the U. Place the 10-in. wire in the middle of the two legs of the U, with about 1 1/4 in. extending above the marks **(photo a)**. Make sure that there are narrow spaces (about 1/16 in.) between the wires. Tape all the wires together on the U side of the bundle, making sure you don't cover up the marks.

2 Working off the spool, wrap the 26-gauge wire two or three times around the middle frame wire slightly above the marks, and then start weaving. Weave three or four times.

3 Maintaining even spacing between the wires, shape the first wave by bending the 16-gauge wires into a gentle curve **(photo b)**.

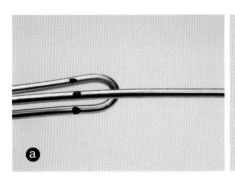
(a)

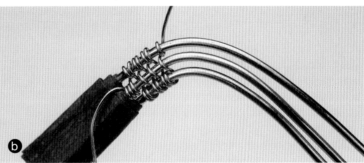
(b)

Add pearls and crystals within the wave to make a playful, freeform pin.

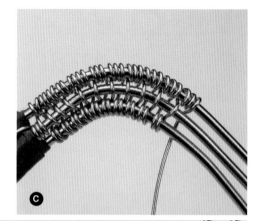

4 Continue weaving, adding an extra wrap between the weaves at the top of the curve **(photo c)**. When you have woven about ¾ of the first wave, shape the next wave going in the opposite direction **(photo d)**.

5 Continue weaving and shaping the waves until you reach the desired length **(photo e)**. Wrap the weaving wire two or three times around the middle frame wire and trim the end.

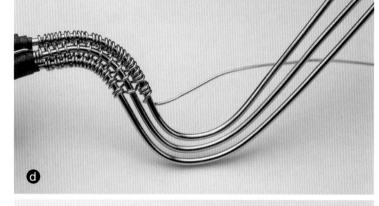

NOTE:
Randomly spaced waves give the bracelet more character than weaves that are all the same size.

Make the hook

6 Bend the end of the middle frame wire toward the top of the bracelet until it lies flat against the weave. Bend the two side wires toward each other until they cross in the middle. Mark both wires at the cross-section. Using flatnose pliers, grab the bottom wire at the mark and bend it slightly to run straight out from the center of the ribbon. Bend the other wire to run perpendicular to the first wire **(photo f)**. Wrap the top wire around the base of the bottom wire two or three times. Trim the wire, making sure the cut end is on the bottom. Cut the other wire end to ¾ in. Using needlenose pliers, make a small loop at the end of the wire, looping it toward the top of the bracelet **(photo g)**. Using roundnose pliers, shape

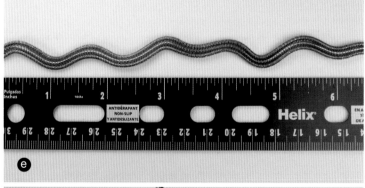

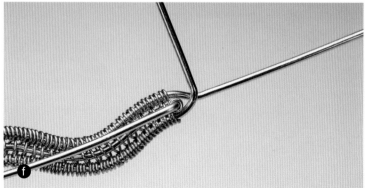

the hook in the opposite direction of the loop you just made **(photo h)**.

7 Trim the tail of the weaving wire on the other end of the bracelet, and remove the tape. To center the clasp's loop, place round-nose pliers inside the loop and twist the pliers in the direction you want it to bend **(photo i)**.

8 Trim both ends of the middle frame wire to equal lengths of about 1 in. beyond the end of the woven section. Use these ends to make decorative spirals. Texture the swirls by setting them on a steel bench block and striking them with a hammer (optional) **(photo j)**. Push them tightly against the body of the bracelet.

9 Shape your bracelet by curving it around a bracelet mandrel or other rounded object.

10 Apply liver of sulfur solution (optional). Tumble for 20 minutes or longer.

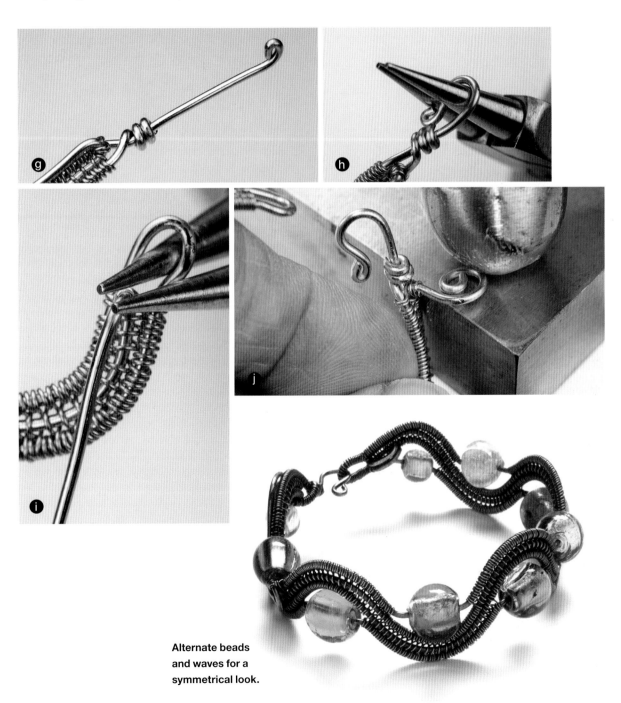

Alternate beads and waves for a symmetrical look.

Over-Over Weave

The over-over weave is a close relative to the over-under weave. Even though they are different, both of these weaves can be employed in similar fashion and can often be used interchangeably. In fact, the projects included in the over-under weave section could be completed with the over-over weave with slightly different results.

The most significant difference between the two weaves (and what gives each its distinctive look) is the path the weaving wire travels as it weaves around the frame wires. In over-under weave, the weaving wire crosses the gaps between frame wires as it alternates between being on top of and then under each frame wire. This creates a checkerboard grid that binds all the wires together. In over-over weave, on the other hand, the weaving wire travels over the frame wires two at a time and then loops around each one separately, locking them in a tight grip of these loops.

techniques

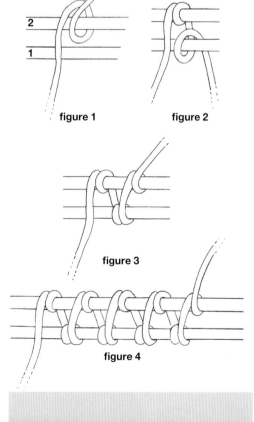

figure 1   figure 2

figure 3

figure 4

(a)

Basic double over-over weave
This weave is made with two frame wires running parallel to each other with space between them equal to at least double the thickness of the weaving wire (just like in over-under weave).

To start the over-over weave, the weaving wire first travels over frame wires 1 and 2 and loops around frame wire 2 **(figure 1)**. After the loop is pulled tightly against frame wire 2, the weaving wire turns around and (now from the back) travels over frame wires 2 and 1 and loops around frame wire 1 **(figure 2)**. Next, it turns to again go over frame wires 1 and 2, and loops around frame wire 2 **(figure 3)**. This pattern continues for as long as desired **(figure 4, photo a)**.

Basic three-wire over-over weave
Again, just like in the over-under weave this three-wire over-over weave is done with three frame wires (marked 1, 2, and 3 in figures 5–8) running parallel to one another with spaces between each two equal to at least double the thickness of the weaving wire. As in the double weave, in the three-wire weave, the weaving wire starts by traveling over frame wires 1 and 2 and looping around frame wire 2. Instead of turning as it would in the double weave, the weaving wire continues up over frame wires 2 and 3, and then loops around frame wire 3 **(figure 5)**.

At this point, the weaving wire makes a U-turn and (from the back) travels over frame wires 3 and 2, loops around frame wire 2, goes over frame wires 2 and 1, and loops around frame wire 1 **(figure 6)**. Next, it makes a U-turn and (in the front again) travels over frame wires 1 and 2, loops around frame wire 2, goes over frame wires 2 and 3, and loops

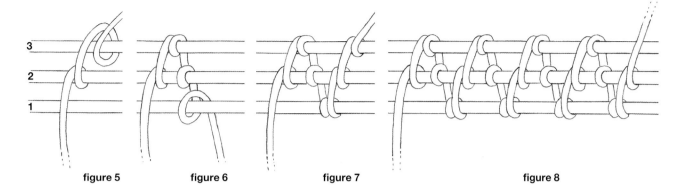

figure 5   **figure 6**   **figure 7**   **figure 8**

around frame wire 3 **(figure 7)**. Continue in this fashion for as long as desired **(figure 8** and **photo b)**.

Four and more wire weaves

The over-over weaving technique for weaving with four or more frame wires is the same as weaving with two or three wires. All you have to do is follow the same over-over pattern for any number of frame wires: The weaving wire goes over frame wires 1 and 2, loops around 2, goes over 2 and 3, loops around 3, goes over 3 and 4, loops around 4, and so on until all the frame wires are used up. At the end of each weave-across, the weaving wire makes a complete loop and it turns to start the next row **(photo c)**.

Creating patterns

The over-over weave can be used to create patterned ribbons. In basic weaves, the weaving wire runs continuously across all the frame wires resulting in a very uniform, unchanging pattern. By varying the number of wraps between the weaves and by selectively excluding portions of frame wires from the weave, you can create countless other patterns. The patterns can be repeating or non-repeating.

For a repeating pattern, create a sequence of different weaves and then repeat that sequence over and over. For example, when working with a four-wire ribbon, I created a simple sequence by first weaving across all four wires for two turns and then, excluding two wires at the top, weaving across the two bottom wires for five turns. As I repeated that sequence several times, one after another, I created a repeating pattern **(photo d)**. This pattern would be described as a repeating pattern of two weaves across all the wires, five weaves across two bottom wires. The sequence can be simple or complex; as long as it repeats, it is a repeating pattern **(photo e)**.

The patterns can also be made intentionally random where different segments of the weave are arranged in no particular order. These are non-repeating patterns. They are usually spontaneous, created without a formula **(photo f)**.

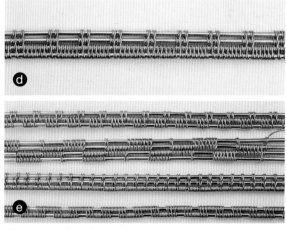

Four-wire (top) and six-wire (bottom) basic weave.

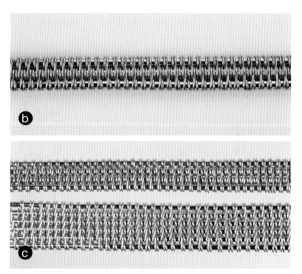

More examples of repeating patterns.

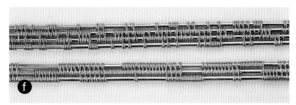

Examples of non-repeating patterns.

Ribbon
bracelet

The bracelet design in this project demonstrates a beautiful application for a simple woven ribbon. This extremely versatile design can easily be adapted to create a wide variety of other bracelets. Just by changing the number of frame wires in the ribbon, you can adjust the width of the bracelet from very narrow to very wide. You can also use many different weave patterns to create countless other design options. Try wires of different gauges, as well as various combinations of round and square wires for more variety.

Skills to review:
**balling up wire, p. 19, stitching,
p. 22, over-over weave, p 40,
creating patterns, p. 41**

Tools

- Weaving tools
- Hot tools
- Patina tools and supplies (optional)
- Finishing tools and supplies
- Bail-making pliers

Materials

5½–6½ (7–8, 8½–9½ in.) bracelet*

- 16 in. (17 in., 18 in.) 18-gauge square half-hard wire
- 30 in. (33 in., 36 in.) 18-gauge round dead-soft wire
- 2½ ft. 26-gauge dead-soft wire for every inch of weaving**
- 2 18-gauge 3mm inside diameter jump rings (or similar size)

* Measurements for larger sizes listed in parentheses.

** Determine the length of your ribbon in Prepare the Frame Wires, step 4.

Prepare the frame wires

1 Trim 3 in. from the total length of the square wire and set the 3-in. piece aside.

2 Mark the centerpoint of the 13-in. square wire, and then mark ⅛ in. on both sides of the centerpoint. Place the edge of your flatnose pliers at one of the ⅛-in. marks, and bend the wire 90°.

NOTE:

Make sure you are grasping the wire's flat sides, not the corners.

Bend the wire 90° at the other ⅛-in. mark in the same direction as the first bend, forming a squared U. Mark both wire ends ¼ in. from the bottom corner of the U **(photo a)**.

3 Cut the round 18-gauge wire into three equal pieces. Mark ½ in. from one end of each of these wires. Place all three wires in the middle of the U-shaped wire, lining up the marks on all the wires. Make sure there are about ¹⁄₁₆-in. spaces between all the wires, and tape the bundle together on the U end just above the marks **(photo b)**.

4 Figure out the length of the ribbon you will need to weave by subtracting ¾ in. (the length needed for the clasp) from your bracelet size. Measure that length from the marks at the bottom of the U, and mark the length of the ribbon across all the wires.

Weave the ribbon

5 Leaving a 4-in. tail, use the 26-gauge wire to weave the length of the ribbon using over-over weave. Start with three weaves across all the wires, then use a repeating pattern of six weaves across the three middle wires and two weaves across alll five wires. End with three weaves across all the wires. Trim the wire, leaving a 4-in. tail **(photo c)**.

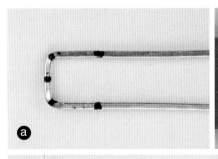

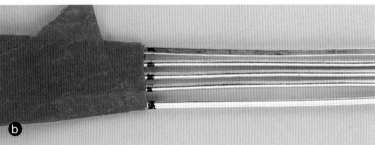

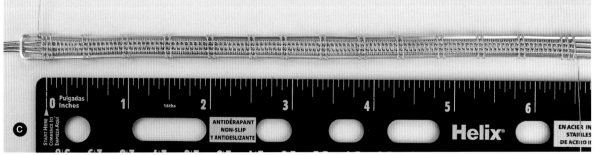

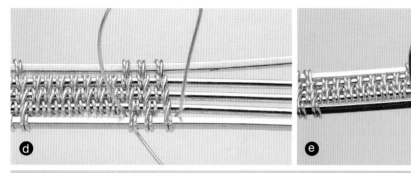

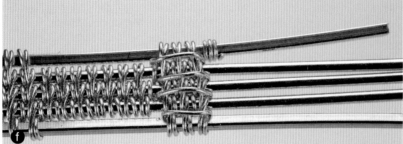

6 Working at one end of the ribbon: Slip the 4-in. tail between the first and second frame wire to bring it to the front, and then thread it down between the same two frame wires, just beyond the last three weaves of the ribbon **(photo d)**. Pull the tail down until the wire lies flat against the weave. Bring the tail back to the front, this time between the second and third frame wires at the end of the weave, and then thread it down through the space beyond the last three weaves again **(photo e)**. Continue in this pattern until you have four wraps around the last three weaves, one for each space between the frame wires. Wrap the tail wire around the last frame wire a few times, and trim **(photo f)**. Repeat on the other ribbon end. (This wrap is optional, but it will give the bracelet a nice finish.)

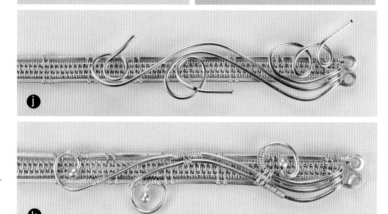

NOTE:
You can use the needle tool to enlarge the spaces between the frame wires.

Shape the frame wire ends

7 At the end of the bracelet that has the U-bend, trim the short ends of the middle three frame wires to equal pieces of about ⅜ in. beyond the end of the weave. With flatnose pliers, grasp across the tips of the wires (no more than about ⅛ in. from the ends), and bend the tips slightly down

toward the underside of the bracelet **(photo g)**. Push the wires all the way down until the bent ends rest against the body of the bracelet **(photo h)**.

8 At the other end of the bracelet, bend the middle wires up and over until they lie flat against the top of the bracelet. Trim the ends of the square wires to ⅜ in. beyond the end of the weave. Using roundnose pliers, make small loops, bending them toward the center of the bracelet **(photo i)**.

9 Shape the three middle wires into decorative squiggles.

NOTE:

You can make these squiggles any way you want them: big, small, wide, narrow, curved, or angular. You can also omit them completely and finish the wires the way you did on the other end of the bracelet.

Mark where you want the squiggles to end, and then measure ⅜ in. (the length of wire needed to make a balled end) from that mark and trim the wires at that point **(photo j)**. Pull the wires away from the bracelet, and ball up each end. Reshape the wires, making any last-minute adjustments and changes. Secure the wires to the bracelet's body using stitching techniques **(photo k)**.

Make the hook

10 Mark the centerpoint and ⅜ in. from each end of the 3-in. square wire. With roundnose pliers, where the jaw measures ⅛ in. diameter, grasp the wire at its centerpoint. Loop both ends around until they cross at the ⅜-in. marks **(photo l)**. Using flatnose pliers, bend the wires slightly outward at the marks. Using the roundnose pliers, make small loops the same size as the loops in step 7 **(photo m)**.

11 With flatnose pliers, grasp across the U-bend (rounded tip) about ⅛ in. from the end, and bend it slightly down **(photo n)**.

12 Using medium-sized bail-making pliers, grasp across the wires about ⅓ of the way down from the bent-up end. Hold onto the looped ends, and twist the pliers to wrap the wires around the smaller (⅛ in.) barrel and shape the hook **(photo o)**.

13 Connect the hook to the bracelet with two jump rings **(photo p)**.

Finish

14 Shape the bracelet using a bracelet mandrel or other rounded object.

15 Apply liver of sulfur solution (optional). Tumble for 20 minutes or longer.

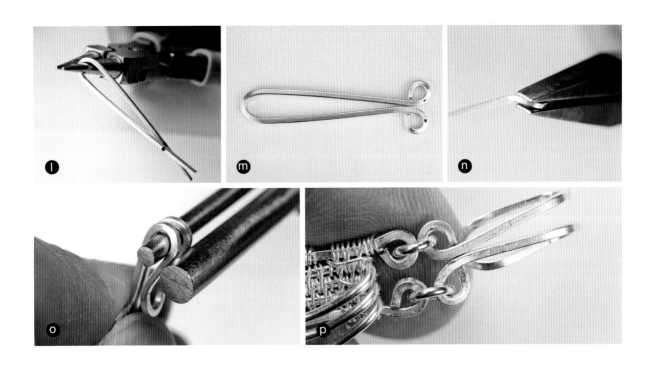

Twisted Ribbon
earrings

This project is a twist (literally) on the ribbon concept. Here, a single woven strip is folded and twisted together to create a new, more dimensional ribbon. Notice how twisting the ribbon not only changes the shape of that ribbon, but also alters the apparent pattern of the weave?

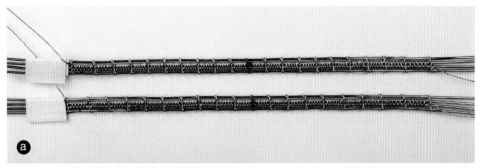

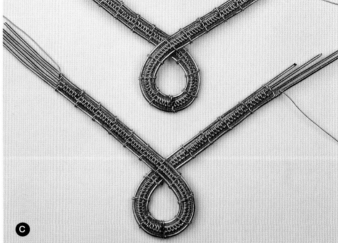

Skills to review:
filing, p. 18, stitching on beads: method #3, p. 23, over-over weave, p. 40

Tools

- Weaving tools
- Patina tools and supplies (optional)
- Finishing tools and supplies
- ¼-in. diameter dowel
- Table vise

Materials

- 4 ft. 20-gauge half-hard wire
- 16 ft. 28-gauge dead-soft wire
- 6 in. 26-gauge wire
- 2 8mm beads
- Pair of earring post backs

1 Cut the 20-gauge wire into eight 6-in. pieces. Make two bundles of four wires each. Mark 1 in. from one end of each bundle, and tape the wires together just outside the mark. Starting at the 1-in. marks, weave each ribbon with 28-gauge wire. Use the over-over weave with a repeating pattern of six weaves across two middle wires and one weave across all three wires to weave a 4-in. section on each ribbon. Mark the centerpoint of each ribbon **(photo a)**.

2 Clamp a ¼-in dowel in a vise. Place the center of the woven section of one of the ribbons on its edge on the underside of the dowel. Bring the ends of the ribbon up and around the dowel until they cross above the dowel **(photo b)**. Repeat for the second earring, making the ends cross in the opposite direction from the first earring **(photo c)**.

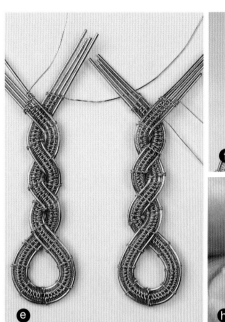

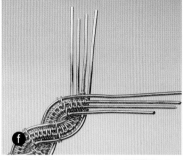

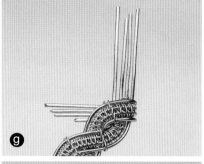

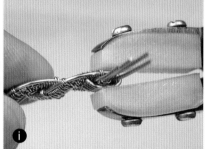

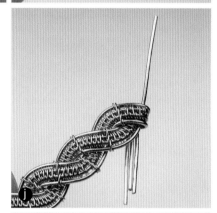

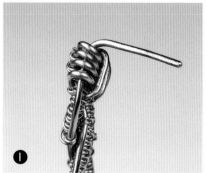

3 Bend the ends of one of the ribbons toward one another until they cross again (this time in the other direction) to create the first twist right above the loop. Repeat for the second ribbon **(photo d)**.

NOTE:

For even bends, work slowly and in several steps; switch back and forth, bending each ribbon only slightly each time.

---

4 Create two more twists **(photo e)**.

5 Working with one earring, unravel any weaving that extends beyond the last twist. Trim the tail ends of the weaving wire **(photo f)**.

6 Bend the wire ends of the top ribbon toward the back of the earring **(photo g)**. Trim the wires to about ¼ in., and then file the ends at a 45° angle.

7 Grasp all four wire tips with flat-nose pliers and bend them slightly down **(photo h)**. Use nylon-jaw pliers

to press the wire ends all the way down to lie flat against the earring **(photo i)**.

8 Bend three of the four wire ends of the other ribbon back, leaving the end closest to the center straight. This wire will become the earring's post **(photo j)**.

9 Trim the three bent wire ends to ¼ in. File the ends at a 45° angle, bend the tips, and push them down to lay on top of and at a 90° angle to the wire ends of the other ribbon **(photo k)**.

10 Trim the post wire to ⅜ in., file the end smooth, and then bend at a 90° angle to the earring **(photo l)**.

11 Attach an 8mm bead in the center of the loop with 3 in. of 26-gauge wire (see Stitching on Beads: Method #3, p. 23).

12 Repeat steps 5–11 for the second earring.

13 Apply liver of sulfur solution (optional). Tumble for 20 minutes.

Filigree
pendant

Filigree is created by arranging small wire components into intricate patterns and connecting them together. With traditional filigree work, the components are soldered. In woven filigree, they are held together with short sections of weaves. I like to use over-over weave for this purpose because it creates strong bonds. This necklace was designed with just four wire elements that are fairly large; to create more complex and ornate patterns, use a greater number of smaller components.

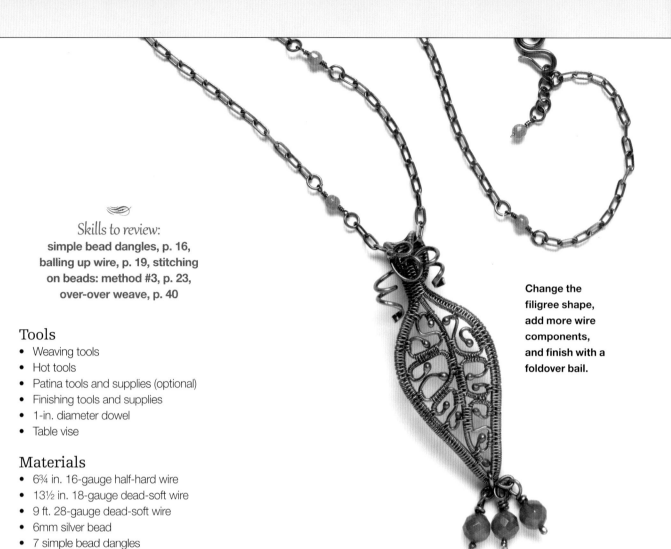

Skills to review:
simple bead dangles, p. 16,
balling up wire, p. 19, stitching
on beads: method #3, p. 23,
over-over weave, p. 40

Tools
- Weaving tools
- Hot tools
- Patina tools and supplies (optional)
- Finishing tools and supplies
- 1-in. diameter dowel
- Table vise

Materials
- 6¾ in. 16-gauge half-hard wire
- 13½ in. 18-gauge dead-soft wire
- 9 ft. 28-gauge dead-soft wire
- 6mm silver bead
- 7 simple bead dangles

Change the
filigree shape,
add more wire
components,
and finish with a
foldover bail.

Shape the frame wires

1 Cut the 18-gauge wire into 3½-in., 4½-in. and 5½-in. pieces. Ball up both ends of all the wires, including the 6¾-in. 16-gauge wire.

2 Find the centerpoint of the 16-gauge wire, and measure and mark 2 in. on either side of the centerpoint. Shape the outer frame of the pendant by wrapping the 16-gauge wire around the 1-in. dowel until its ends cross at the 2-in. marks **(photo a)**. Remove the frame from the dowel. Place the jaw of the flatnose pliers at each 2-in. mark, and bend the wires out until they no longer cross **(photo b)**. Use the balled-up ends to create mirror-image spirals on both sides of the pendant **(photo c)**.

3 Using the 5½-in. piece of 18-gauge wire, form an S shape to fit inside and to the left of the frame created in step 2. This shape should take up more than half of the space. Using the 3½-in. piece of 18-gauge wire, create a second S shape to fit in the leftover space next to the first S **(photo d)**.

4 Mark the jaw of the roundnose pliers where it measures about ⅛ in. in diameter. Mark the jaw three more times, making the second mark slightly below the first one, the third below the second, and the fourth below the third. Find and mark the centerpoint of the 4½-in. piece of 18-gauge wire. Grasp the wire with the roundnose pliers, lining up the centerpoint of the wire with the uppermost mark on the jaw of the pliers. Wrap the ends of the wire around the jaw to create a loop **(photo e)**. Measure to make sure that the ends of the wire extending to either side of the loop are exactly the same length. Adjust the position of the loop.

Use the roundnose pliers to grasp the wire on one side of the loop and right next to it. Line up the wire with the second mark on the pliers. Form the second loop. Repeat on the other side **(photo f)**. Create two more loops on each side using the third and fourth marks on the pliers, making each loop a little smaller than the one before it. When all the loops are done, the balled-up ends should extend slightly beyond the last loops. Adjust the curve of the looped wire to match the curve at the bottom of the pendant's frame **(photo g)**.

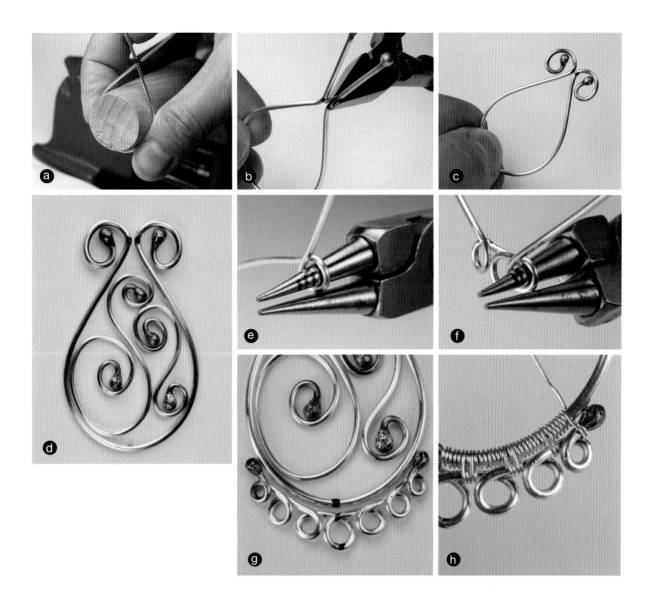

Weave the parts together

5 Align the frame and the looped wire's center marks, and then tape the two shapes together to the left of the center marks. Cut a 3½-ft. piece of 28-gauge wire. Wrap the wire four or five times around the pendant's frame wire at its centerpoint. Using basic over-over weave, weave twice in the space between the first and the second loop. Wrap the weaving wire around the frame wire again until you reach the next space between the loops. Weave twice, wrap again, and then weave one time between the last two loops. Wrap again, and place one weave just below the bead at the end of the looped wire **(photo h)**.

6 Replace the S shapes inside the frame, and mark the points where they come in contact with the frame **(photo i)**.

7 Continue weaving on the right side, attaching the smaller S shape in the places indicated by the marks on the frame. Use the three-wire over-over weaving technique to weave the S-shape and the frame at the same time. Stop weaving before the last mark. Do not trim the wire **(photo j)**.

Use back-to-back filigrees to create a gorgeous ring.

8 Cut another 3½-ft. piece of 28-gauge wire. Start in the center, and weave to the left and toward the top the same way you did on the right side. In places where the large S shape overlaps the looped wire, use the three-wire over-over weaving technique to weave them and the frame all at the same time **(photo k)**.

9 Continue weaving all the way to the top, incorporating the side swirl in the weave and weaving together the wires at the top of the frame. Switching to the right side again, weave all the way to the top, attaching the top of the large S and the right side swirl **(photo l)**.

10 Cut 2 ft. of 28-gauge wire. Weave down the center of the pendant, connecting the two S shapes together in places where they meet **(photo m)**.

Finish the pendant

11 Attach the 6mm silver bead at the top of the pendant (see Stitching on Beads: Method #3, p. 23).

12 Attach simple bead dangles to the loops at the bottom. Attach a chain and clasp.

13 Apply liver of sulfur solution (optional). Tumble for 20 minutes.

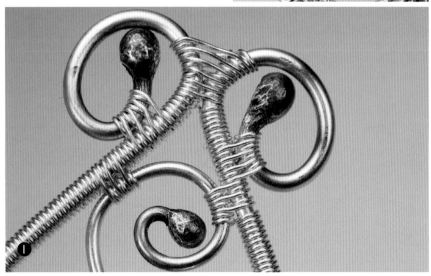
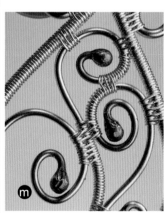

Circular Weave

Circular weaving is very similar to over-under and over-over weaving. The difference is that the circular weave travels in a circular instead of linear motion, and it is a continuous weave that does not turn around at the edges, the way it does in the linear weaves. With circular weave, you can create flat shapes such as circles, squares, and ovals, as well as three-dimensional forms like baskets, cones, and cylinders.

techniques

Flat circular weave

Flat circular weave uses a set of spokes radiating from the center in a star-like formation as a frame. The best way to create the frame is to line up several frame wires, bind them in the middle, and then spread the ends out evenly to create the star shape. There are several ways of binding the wires. Here are two that I like to use:

Method #1: The center is woven with the basic over-over weave. This is my favorite bind; it results in a nice, flat center and has an easy transition into the circular weave.

1 Cut the number of frame wires required for the project and line them up. Find and mark the centerpoint of the wire, and then weave one or two times across the middle wires slightly to the left of the centerpoint. Next, weave twice across all the wires, and then weave one or two times across the middle wires to the right of center **(photo a)**.

NOTE:
The wider you make the center weave, the more oval the finished shape will be.

---

2 Spread the wires apart and arrange them evenly around the center. Continue weaving with the same wire you used for binding, switching to one of the circular weaves **(photo b)**.

Method #2: The center is bound with a cross-wrap. I like to use this bind when working with six or more frame wires that would result in too broad of a center when bound with Method #1.

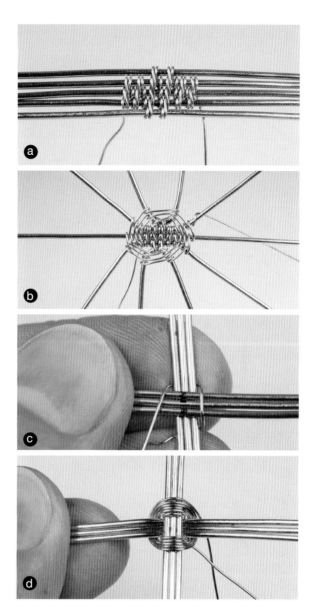

1 Divide the wires to be used into two sets with an equal number of wires in each set. Find and mark the center point of each set. Place one set on top of the other at a 90° angle with the centerpoints lining up, forming a cross.

2 Starting left of center, run the weaving wire over the top set of wires. Moving clockwise, bring the weaving wire under the wires that are extending up, then over the wires to the right of center and under the wires extending down **(photo c)**.

3 Continue wrapping the weaving wire in this fashion until you have a few wraps around the center. Make sure the wraps are tight and remain flat against the frame wires **(photo d)**.

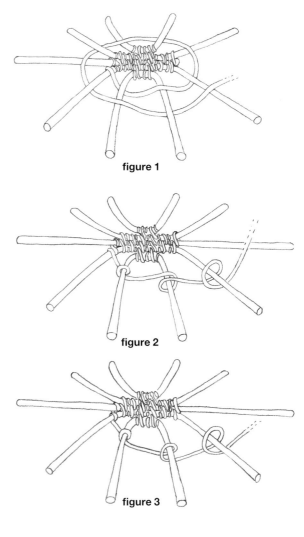

figure 1

Odd number of frame wires (left), even number of frame wires (right).

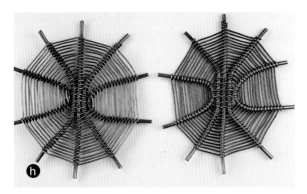

figure 2

figure 3

4 Spread the frame wires apart and arrange them evenly around the center. Continuing with the same wire you used for the bind, start weaving with one of the circular weaves **(photo e)**.

Types of flat circular weave

Over-under basket weave: This is the common basket weave where the weaving wire alternates going over and under each spoke. This method works only with an odd number of spokes. In the flat circular weave, where each frame wire creates two spokes, you always start with even number of spokes. To get to the uneven number, you will need to bend one of the frame wire ends out of the way **(figure 1, photo f)**.

Over-under looping weave: Here, the weaving wire also travels over and under each spoke like in the basket weave. However, in the looping technique, the weaving wire loops around each spoke every time it goes by.

This weave produces two distinctly different patterns depending on whether you're using an even or odd number of spokes **(figure 2, photo g)**.

Over-over weave: The third method uses the over-over technique. This is the most consistent weave and produces the same pattern with any number of spokes. Unlike the other circular weaves, that look the same on both sides, this one has a smooth pattern on one side and a ribbed one on the other side **(figure 3, photo h)**.

From flat to three-dimensional weave

If you bend the frame wires up or down as you continue weaving, you will create a basket shape and automatically shift into three-dimensional weaving **(photo i)**. If you continue bringing the frame wires closer and closer together and bend them up to run parallel to each other, you will eventually be weaving a cylindrical shape **(photo j)**.

Cylindrical weave

Cylindrical weave uses parallel frame wires arranged in a circular fashion, like a tube or a cylinder. It follows the same patterns as flat circular weaves. To start the cylindrical weave, line up the frame wires in a flat bundle and tape them together at one end **(photo k)**. Weave once across all the wires with over-over weave.

NOTE:

Using over-over weave is the easiest way to start the cylindrical weave. After the first weave, you can switch to whatever weave pattern you will be using for the main part. At the end, you can remove the first weave if you wish.

Roll the wires into a cylinder. Connect the last wire to the first with the next weave **(photo l)**. Continue weaving using one of the circular weaves **(photo m)**.

From cylindrical weave to flat weave

To transition from cylindrical to flat weave, simply bend the frame wires at a 90° angle, and then continue weaving **(photo n)**. If you wish, from here you can transition to the basket shape and then back to the cylinder.

Adding beads

There are two easy ways to add beads to circular weave:

Method #1: String the beads on the wire spokes. The beads must be small enough to fit side by side around the circle. When you reach the area where you want to add beads, wrap the weaving wire a couple of times around one of the spokes and trim. String a bead on each spoke. Start a new wire to resume weaving **(photo o)**.

Method #2: When you reach the area where you want to start adding beads, string a bead on the weaving wire. Let the bead slip into the space between two spokes, and then weave around the next spoke. String another bead, weave the wire around the next spoke, and continue on until you complete the circle. Resume regular weaving **(photo p)**.

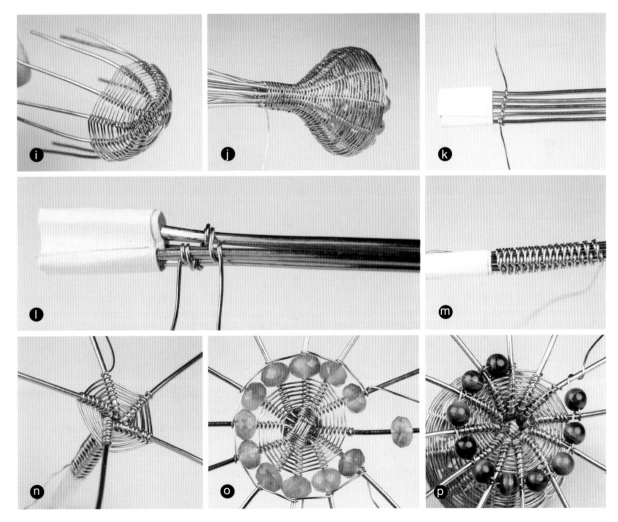

In Full Bloom
bracelet and earrings

Sometimes a single something can look ordinary, but put together several somethings, and you create a showpiece! That is the case with this bracelet. In this design, you'll string together a number of identical components crafted using basic circular weave. Because you're repeating the same woven element over and over, by the time you are finished with this project, you should have a good grasp of the basic circular weave.

Tools

- Weaving tools
- Hot tools
- Finishing tools and supplies
- Patina tools and supplies (optional)

NOTE:

Each finished flower has an approximately 1¼ in. diameter. To adjust the length of your bracelet, vary the number of flowers; change the sizes and number of jump rings used to connect the components; or adjust the clasp size.

Materials

- 11⅔ ft. 20-gauge half-hard wire
- 14 yd. 28-gauge dead-soft wire
- 21 in. 26-gauge dead-soft wire
- 7 6–8mm beads
- 24 or more 20-gauge 1¹⁄₆₄-in. inside diameter jump rings (or similar size)
- Clasp (purchased or woven; see p. 32)
- Pair of ear wires

NOTE:

You may need a few more jump rings, depending on the method you use for attaching the clasp.

Bracelet

1 Cut the 20-gauge wire into 4-in. pieces, five for each flower. Ball up each end of each 4-in. wire. Make the balls fairly large; after the balls are formed, the wires should shrink from 4 in. to about 2¾ in. Measure and mark the centerpoint of each wire.

2 Place five of the wires side by side, lining up their centerpoints, and then tape them together at one end. Cut a 6-ft. piece of 28-gauge wire (or work off the spool). Using Flat Circular Weave: Method #1, p. 53, weave the wires together at the center. Remove the tape, separate the ends of the frame wires, and arrange them into a star-like formation. Continuing with the same wire used for weaving the center, start weaving around the circle. Hold the circle with nylon-jaw pliers as you work. Weave until the woven circle is about 1 in. in diameter (12 or 13 times around) **(photo a)**. If you are working off the spool, cut off the weaving wire, leaving a 12-in. tail.

3 Grasp the end (right below the ball) of one of the frame wires with the tip of the chainnose pliers. Twist the wire down toward the center of the woven

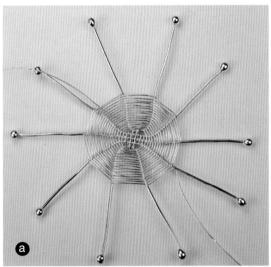

(a)

b

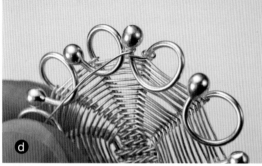

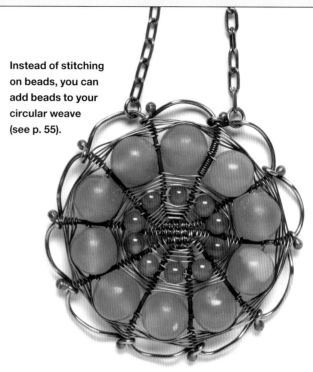

Instead of stitching on beads, you can add beads to your circular weave (see p. 55).

circle, then up, forming a loop **(photo b)**. The loop should overlap the woven section a bit, and the ball at the end of the wire should extend slightly beyond the woven area. Do the same with the rest of the frame wires **(photo c)**.

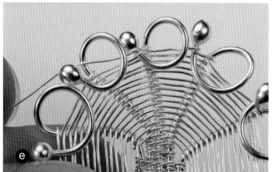

4 Using the tail end of the weaving wire, weave once more all the way around the circle. This time, incorporate the balled-up wire ends into the weave **(photos d, e)**. Repeat all the way around, securing all the loops in place. Wrap the end of the weaving wire a couple of times around the last frame wire, and trim the end.

5 Cut a 3-in. piece of 26-gauge wire, and attach the bead in the middle of the flower (see Stitching on Beads: Method #1, p. 22).

6 Repeat steps 2–5 for the other flowers.

7 Connect the flowers with jump rings **(photo f)**. Attach the clasp with jump rings.

8 Apply liver of sulfur solution (optional). Tumble for 20 minutes or more.

Earrings

1 Repeat steps 1–5 of "Bracelet" to make two flowers.

2 Attach ear wires to complete the earrings. Apply liver of sulfur solution and tumble (optional).

Gnarly
bangle

Unlike most of the other designs in this chapter, which require exact measurements, this bracelet is almost completely freeform. All wire lengths listed in the supply list are approximate. If, for example, you wish to add extra twists to your bracelet's band or more wraps around the band, use frame wires that are a bit longer. Similarly, the amount of weaving wire used will depend on the density and length of your weave.

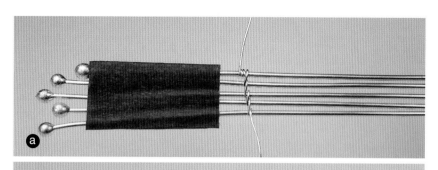

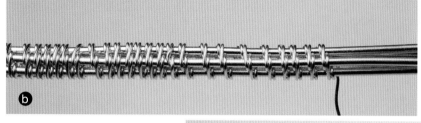

This bracelet uses a half-looped cage to hold a bead (see p. 71).

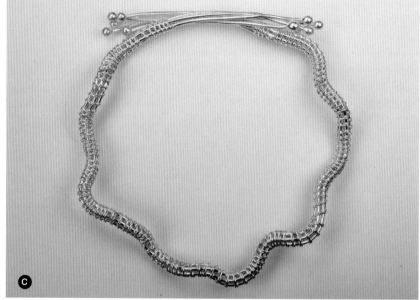

Skills to review:
**balling up wire, p. 19,
stitching, p. 22, stitching on
beads: method #3, p. 23,
circular weave: cylindrical
weave, p. 54**

Tools
- Weaving tools
- Hot tools
- Finishing tools and supplies
- Patina tools and supplies (optional)
- Bracelet mandrel

Materials
- 100–110 in. 18-gauge dead-soft wire
- 20–25 ft. 26-gauge dead-soft wire
- 4–6 6–8mm beads

1 Cut the 18-gauge wire into five 12-in. pieces (13–14 in. for a larger bracelet) and one 40-in. piece. Ball up both ends of each wire.

2 Line up the five shorter wires with their balled-up ends slightly uneven. Tape the ends together, leaving about ¹⁄₁₆-in. spaces between the wires. Start weaving with 26-gauge wire about 1½ in. from one end. Weave once across all the wires **(photo a)**, and then roll the wires into a cylindrical shape.

3 Continue weaving. For added interest, vary the density of the weave: Let the frame wires show in some areas and be completely covered by the weave in others **(photo b)**. Finish weaving about 1½ in. before the end of the frame wires.

4 Bend and twist the entire length of the woven tube to resemble a twisted twig. Shape the tube into a circle. Let the balled-up ends overlap each other by 2–2½ in. **(photo c)**.

5 Wrap the 40-in. piece of wire around the bracelet: Line up one end of the 40-in. wire with the balled-up ends on the

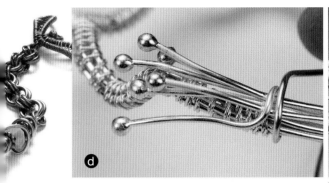

d

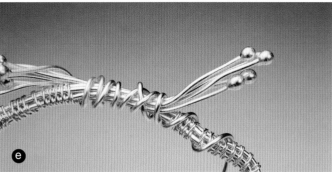

e

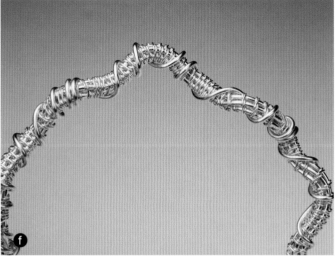

f

left side of the bracelet. Start wrapping about ½–¾ in. from the balled-up ends of the wires **(photo d)**. Wrap several times around the section between the two overlapping ends of the bracelet. When you are about ½–¾ in. from the balled-up ends on the right, lift these ends slightly up and continue wrapping around the bracelet **(photo e)**. Space the wraps out in a random fashion **(photo f)**. Wrap the whole length of the bracelet. When you get back to the top, wrap around the overlap a few more times, ending on the right. Line up the balled-up end of the wrapping wire with the wire ends on the right side of the bracelet **(photo g)**.

6 Fan out and bend up the balled-up ends to give them some character **(photo h)**. Stitch the wire ends with 26-gauge wire in a few places to prevent them from getting caught on clothing. Attach a few beads to the wires at the top of the bracelet (see Stitching on Beads: Method #3, p. 23). Use the needle tool to lift wires and pass the weaving wire under them **(photo i)**.

7 Apply liver of sulfur solution (optional). Tumble for 20 minutes or longer.

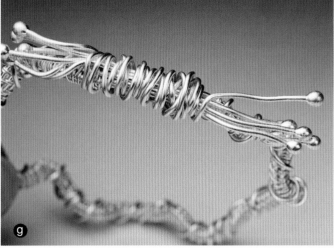

g

h

i

Coiling

Coiling is a relatively easy technique that, when used creatively, can produce stunning results. In its most basic form, a coil is simply a weaving wire wrapped several times around a core (frame) wire. Coiling is often used in conjunction with other weaving methods for filling in spaces between weaves and for adding texture to unwoven sections of frame wires. In addition, single coiled wires can be shaped and twisted into different configurations and used in earrings, bracelets, and other designs.

True coiling as it is defined here, however, is a separate technique that uses a coil-and-connect method to create more complex two- and three-dimensional shapes. In contrast to the over-under and over-over weaves that are linear (can only expand in two directions), coiled shapes can grow in all directions, all at the same time. This characteristic of coiling, combined with its ability to conform to practically any shape, makes the technique very flexible and adaptable. Coiling can be used as a stand-alone technique, or it can be paired with other weaving methods.

techniques

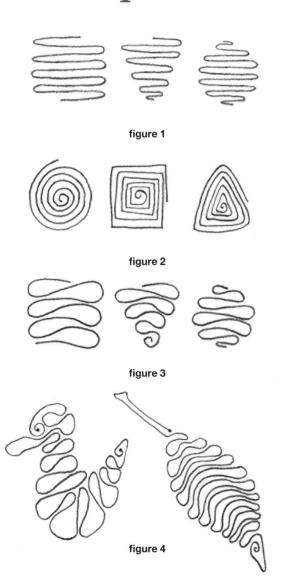

figure 1

figure 2

figure 3

figure 4

Coiled shapes

The best way to create a coiled shape is to use a continuous frame wire and fold it upon itself. There are countless ways of folding the wire, the simplest ones being lined and circular. In lined coiling, the wire is folded, accordion-style **(figure 1)**. In circular coiling, the wire is spiraled around a central point **(figure 2)**.

Coiled wires can fit tightly together creating a solid, unbroken surface when connected, or be shaped into wavy lines with open spaces between them **(figure 3)**, creating lace-like patterns resembling macramé work (see the Heart of Gold Pendant, p. 82).

With some modifications and blending of the lined and circular folding techniques, coiling can be used to create practically any shape you can imagine. If you draw an outline of a flat shape and draw a squiggly line inside the outline that runs from edge to edge and fills the entire space, you can follow that line with wire to create a coiled version of that shape (see the Snail Pendant, p. 68) **(figure 4)**.

Basic coil-and-connect technique

In order for a coiled piece to hold its shape, the folded sections of frame wire need to be connected to each other. The connecting technique is very simple.

In the **lined technique**, coil the first segment of the wire. Fold the frame wire to create the second segment. Coil around and slightly past the bend. Make the first connection by wrapping the weaving wire once or twice around the first and second segment of the coiled wire, coil some more, and make another connection **(figure 5)**. As you continue coiling and folding the wire, make connections at more-

or-less equal intervals. Connect the second row to the first one, the third to the second, the fourth to the third, and so on **(figure 6, photo a)**.

In the **circular technique**, you will need to coil the wire all around the first loop of the spiral, and then make the first connection slightly past the end of the wire **(figure 7)**. Coil the wire some more. Make another connection. Continue coiling and shaping the wire, making attachments at more-or-less equal intervals **(photo b)**.

Adding beads

You can easily add beads to coiled elements by inserting them in the gaps between the coils. To do that, coil and attach the way you normally would. When you get to the spot where you want to insert the bead, bend the frame wire out and back in to make space between the coils. Coil up to where the space is wide enough for the bead you are using, string the bead on the weaving wire, and let it slide into the open space between the coils. Wrap the weaving wire around the coil above the bead twice, and then bring it behind the bead and back to the front **(figures 8, 9)**. Resume regular coiling.

You can add more than one bead into a single space. After finishing with the first bead, coil enough times so that when the second bead is inserted, the two beads fit comfortably side by side. Attach the second bead the same way you did the first one **(figure 10)**.

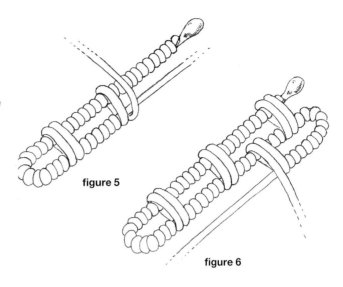

figure 5

figure 6

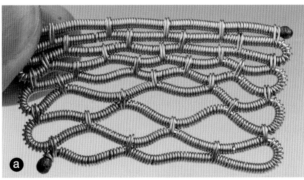

a

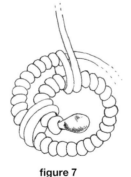

b

figure 7

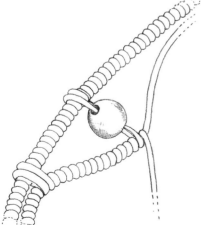

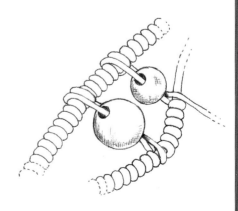

figure 8   figure 9 (back view)   figure 10

Triangular *earrings*

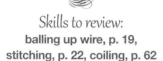

Skills to review:
**balling up wire, p. 19,
stitching, p. 22, coiling, p. 62**

Tools

- Weaving tools
- Hot tools
- Finishing tools and supplies
- Patina tools and supplies (optional)

Materials

- 8½ in. 20-gauge half-hard wire
- 27 in. 18-gauge dead-soft wire
- 22 ft. 28-gauge dead-soft wire
- 32 20-gauge ⅛-in. inside diameter jump rings, or 3 in. of 4–5mm chain and 8 jump rings
- Pair of earring post backs
- 2 simple bead dangles or drops (optional)

Each earring in this project consists of two separate elements: the post that is made using a tightly wound circular coil, and the large triangular dangle made using lined coiling. This gives you the opportunity to practice two different types of coiling techniques. In addition to the way they are used here (connected to form a single earring), the two elements can also be used separately. The triangle, for example can be hung from an ear wire instead of the post, and the earring's post can be used by itself, alone, or with a bead dangle added to it.

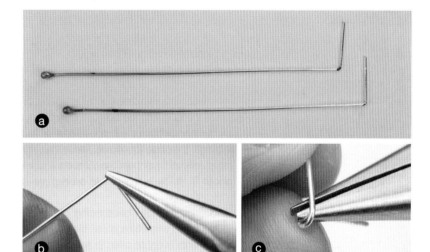

Make coiled posts

1 Cut the 20-gauge wire into two 4¼-in. piece. Ball up one end of each wire. The balls should be approximately the same size. Check to make sure the wires are still of equal length. Trim if necessary.

2 Measure and mark ⅝ in. from the balled ends and ½ in. from the straight ends of both wires. Make a 90° bend in each wire at the ½-in. mark **(photo a)**. Holding one of the wires with the shorter end pointing toward you, grasp across the bend with the tip of your chainnose pliers **(photo b)**, and then loop the longer end up and around the tip of the upper jaw **(photo c)**. Do the same with the other wire, looping it down and around the lower jaw to create a mirror-image loop **(photo d)** of the first wire. These loops are the start of the spirals.

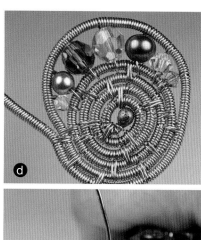

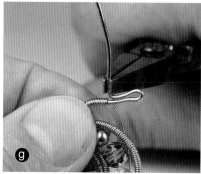

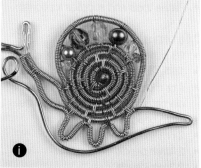

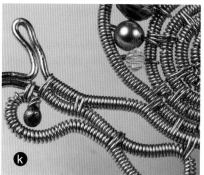

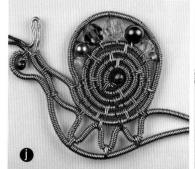

4 Coil around the arc, adding beads in this order: 3mm, 4mm, 6mm, 7mm, 6mm, 4mm, and 3mm. Make an attachment at the end of the arc. Continue to coil and attach the wire around the bottom of the circle to complete the shell part of the snail. Place the last attachment just below the start of the arc. Bend the wire at about 30° and coil it ½ in. **(photo d)**.

5 Mark the wire ⁵⁄₁₆ in. from the end of the coil. Grasp the wire at the mark with the tips of your roundnose pliers, and bend it down around the pliers' jaws to form a small U **(photo e)**.

6 Using flatnose pliers, pinch the wires that you just folded together about ⅛ in. below the U, creating a small loop at the tip. This will become one of the snail's antennae **(photo f)**.

7 Where the wire meets the coiled section, bend it 90° **(photo g)**.

8 Create the second antenna the way you did the first one in steps 5 and 6. Make an attachment just below the antennae, coil 10 times, and make

another attachment. Lay the snail down on a piece of paper and complete its outline by drawing a line for the head, neck, belly, and tail. Shape the wire into several zigzags running up and down between the shell and the part of the line representing the neck and the belly **(photo h)**.

9 Coil and attach the zigzagged wire to the underside of the shell. Shape the wire to complete the rest of the snail. After shaping the head, loop the wire around toward the inside of the head. On the wire, mark where you want the eye to be, and then trim the wire ¼ in. from that mark **(photo i)**.

10 Straighten out the loop, ball up the end, and then reshape the

wire. Coil the tail, the belly, and the neck. Make attachments at the bottom of every zigzag and one attachment at the neck area. Coil around the curve of the head, make an attachment at the base of the antennae, and then coil up to the balled-up wire end. Trim the weaving wire at the base of the ball **(photo j, k)**.

11 Carefully hammer two antennae (just enough to give them some texture). Attach two jump rings between the beads at the top of the shell, and attach two more jump rings to the ones you just added. Attach bead clusters as desired.

12 Apply liver of sulfur solution (optional). Tumble for 20 minutes.

Looping

Looping can be used to create ornamental surfaces, attach beads, and construct bezels and other stone settings. Except for the very first row, where loops must be attached to some kind of a starter frame, looping is done entirely with weaving wire and does not require frame wires.

techniques

Flat (linear) looping

Flat looped elements (nets) are created with straight rows of loops that run back and forth as they are hooked into one another. The first row of loops is attached to a straight piece of frame wire or some other frame material. To start, loop the weaving wire around the frame wire from front to back, and then let it cross in front of its tail as it comes back to the front **(figure 1)**. Make the next loop by bringing the weaving wire around the frame wire from front to back again, then thread it through the space between the first and the second loop **(figure 2)**. Continue looping, spacing the loops evenly until you reach the desired length. After finishing the first row, wrap the starting tail end around the wire of the first loop a couple of times and trim it to finish it off **(figure 3)**. Turn the piece over so that the back is facing you. Start the next row by hooking the first loop of the new row into the last loop of the previous row **(figure 4)**. Continue looping this way, turning the piece over at the end of each row.

Circular looping

Circular looping is similar to linear looping, except the loops travel in a circle in a continuous weave. As you loop, keep the same side toward you and turn the piece around bit by bit so the loops are always at the top. The circular net can grow from the inside out or from the outside in.

From the outside in, as the circle gets larger and the rows get farther from the center, the distance around the circle increases. The same number of loops would become progressively larger. To keep the loops uniform in size, add an extra loop here and there by occasionally hooking two loops into one loop **(figure 5)**.

If the net grows from the outside in, the distance around the circle gets smaller as the rows get closer to the center. Decrease the number of loops by occasionally skipping over a loop here and there **(figure 6)**.

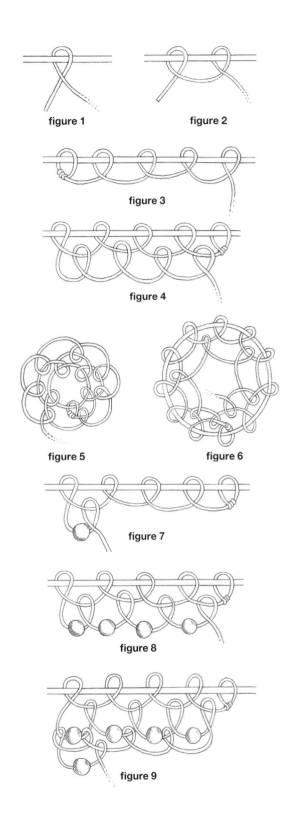

figure 1   figure 2

figure 3

figure 4

figure 5   figure 6

figure 7

figure 8

figure 9

Looping with beads

To add beads to loops, string a bead on the wire and then hook the loop like you normally would **(figure 7)**. You can add a scattering of beads here and there, or weave entire rows of beads **(figure 8)**. For multiple rows, place at least one row of empty loops between the bead rows **(figure 9)**.

Netted
hoop earrings

Because they weigh so little, looped nets are ideal for creating large, showy earrings. Even with the addition of beads, these earrings are usually light enough to be worn by almost anyone. The earrings in this project are round, but you can make looped earrings into practically any shape. Simply build the outer edge of a given shape with frame wire, fill the space inside the rim with loops or beads, and you are done.

Prepare the frame

1 Cut the 18-gauge wire into two 6½-in. pieces. Clamp the dowel in the vise. Bend one of the wires around the dowel until the ends cross at the top. Mark both ends of the wire at the point where they cross **(photo a)**. Repeat for the second wire.

2 Using the 26-gauge weaving wire, coil the sections of the wires between the marks. (You will need about 4½ ft. of wire for each earring.) Bend each 18-gauge wire 90° at one of the marks **(photo b)**.

3 Replace one of the wires on the dowel. Pull it firmly around the dowel making sure the coiled section forms a smooth, even hoop. Wrap the straight end of the wire around the bent end twice **(photo c)**. Trim the end. Repeat for the second earring, wrapping in the opposite direction. Trim the bent end to ⅜ in. above the wrap, and then form a small loop using roundnose pliers.

a

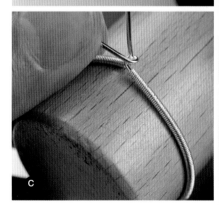

c

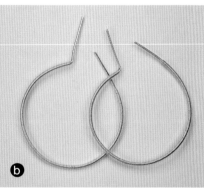

b

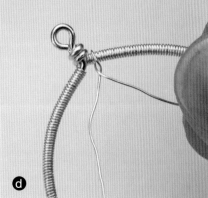

d

Skills to review:
adding wires in looping, p. 22, circular looping, p. 71, looping with beads, p. 71

Tools
- Weaving tools
- Finishing tools and supplies
- Patina tools and supplies (optional)
- 1¾-in.-diameter dowel (or similar size)
- Table vise

Materials
- 13 in. 18-gauge half-hard wire
- 18 ft. 26-gauge dead-soft wire
- 48–50 3mm beads
- 2 12mm flat disk beads with holes across the widest part of the beads
- Pair of ear wires or posts

Loop inside the hoops

4 Cut another 4½-ft. piece of 26-gauge wire (or you can work with shorter sections). Leaving a short tail that you can grasp, make the first loop close to the wrap at the top of the earring **(photo d)**. Loop all around the inside rim of the hoop, spacing the loops about ⅛–³⁄₁₆ in. apart **(photo e)**.

5 Wrap the tail end at the first loop around the weaving wire a couple of times. Trim it. Connect the last loop to the first one, completing the circle **(photo f)**.

6 Continue looping, adding the 3mm beads to the second row of loops **(photo g)**.

NOTE:

Don't worry if the beaded loops do not line up perfectly with the loops in the previous row. It's OK to skip a loop or go into the same loop twice, as long as the beads are spaced evenly.

---

7 Add the next row of loops, looping around the beads **(photo h)**. This time, you should have the same number of loops as there are beads.

8 Continue looping all the way to the center. Remember to occasionally skip loops to reduce the number and keep them about the same size. Do not trim the wire end **(photo i)**.

9 String a 12mm disk bead on the weaving wire **(photo j)**. Attach the wire to a loop at the bottom of the earring **(photo k)**.

10 Repeat steps 4–9 for the second earring.

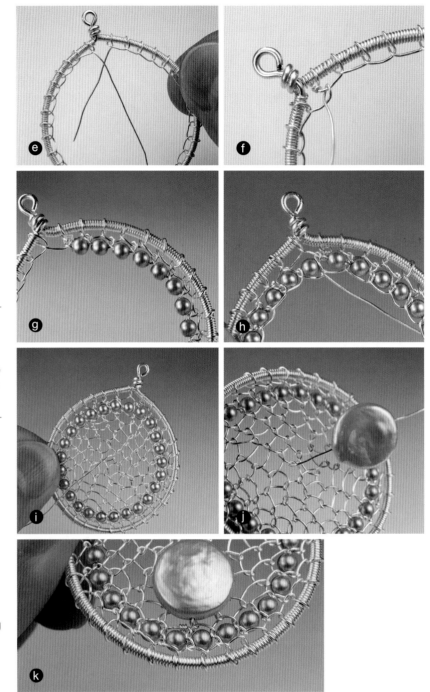

Finish the earrings

11 Attach an ear wire at the top of each earring.

12 Apply liver of sulfur solution (optional). Tumble for 20 minutes.

River Stone
pendant

Looped nets can be molded to follow any contour, which makes them great for encasing different stones—including oddly shaped ones that would be difficult to secure with other methods. Here you will be using what I call three-dimensional circular looping, where loops run in a circle but the looped net grows downward instead of out, creating a "sleeve" to fit the stone. In this technique, the net is molded directly onto the stone's surface, allowing each individual loop to be pulled snug for a net that is as tight as skin and holds the stone in a secure grip.

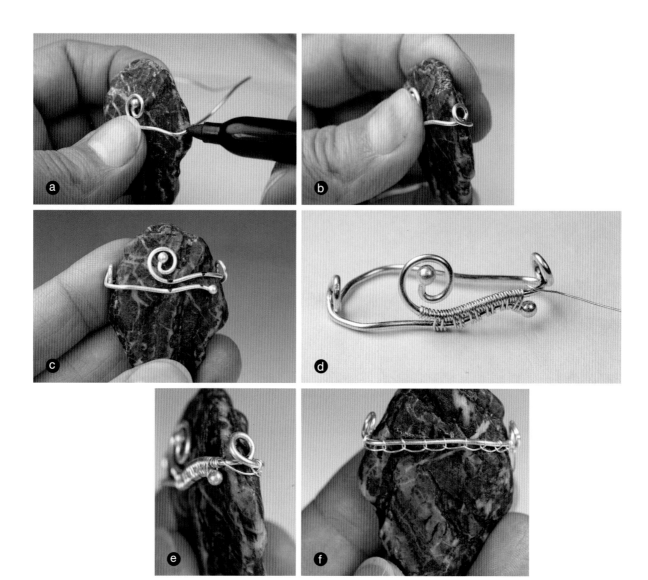

Skills to review:

balling up wire, p. 19, over-over weave, p. 40, flat (linear) looping, p. 71, looping with beads, p. 71

Tools

- Weaving tools
- Finishing tools and supplies
- Patina tools and supplies (optional)

Materials

- 1¼x1¾ in. flat river stone
- 3–5 in. 18-gauge dead-soft wire
- 6–8 ft. 28-gauge dead-soft wire
- 5–6 4mm beads
- Chain and clasp

Note: The stone can be any shape, symmetrical or freeform, but it should be wider in the middle than at either end in order for the net to stay in place.

1 Ball up one end of the 18-gauge wire. Make a small spiral at the balled-up wire end. Hold the spiral against the middle of the front of the stone about a quarter to one-third of the way down from the top (above the widest part of the stone). Bring the wire around to the back. Place a mark where the wire bends at the narrow side of the stone **(photo a)**.

2 With roundnose pliers, make a small loop at the mark **(photo b)**.

3 Holding the loop against the side of the stone, continue wrapping the wire around. Make a second loop at the other narrow side of the stone, and then bring the wire to the front. Let the wire run the whole width of the front of the stone, and then trim the wire about ⅛ in. past the edge of the stone. Bead the end. Mark where the two wire ends overlap in the front **(photo c)**.

4 Remove the wire frame from the stone. Cut a 2–3-ft. piece of 26-gauge wire. Using over-over weave with a repeating pattern of two weaves across two wires and three coils on the top wire, weave between the marks.

Make sure to start at the center and weave toward the edge **(photo d)**.

5 Place the frame back on the stone. Continuing with the same weaving wire, start attaching loops to the frame wire. Loop toward the back of the stone **(photo e)**.

6 Loop across the back **(photo f)**.

7 When you reach the front, again start adding beads to each loop. When you reach the woven section of the frame, place loops on the lower frame wire (use the needle tool to make spaces between the weaves for the weaving wire to pass through). Add enough beads to go all the way across the front of the pendant **(photo g)**.

8 Loop around the back again. Place an empty loop around each bead in the front **(photo h)**.

9 Continue looping around the stone. As you work, use a needle tool to lift the loops slightly away from the stone for easier access. Loop until you get down past the widest part of the stone. End when you are happy with the look **(photos i, j)**.

10 Attach a chain to the frame wire loops on the sides of the stone. Apply liver of sulfur solution (optional). Tumble for 20 minutes or longer.

Chapter 2
The Next Level

This chapter contains a series of projects that demonstrate how the techniques learned in the first part of the book can be expanded and merged to create more advanced and multilevel designs. Here, you will explore more challenging ways of using woven ribbons, interesting techniques for working with beads, and advanced methods for setting stones. The projects will also challenge you to take an active role in the design process by asking you to make some of the creative decisions.

If you have gone through all the lessons and successfully completed most of the projects in the previous chapters, you are ready to tackle any project here in any order. You can complete the designs the way they are presented or modify them using the new skills you've learned.

Looping captures a bone-white shell with striking orange beads.

Crystal
spiral ring

So far, you've used woven ribbons to create flat designs. This project takes the idea of the ribbon in the third dimension. This design is based on a basic knot ring. Simply weave the ribbon without beads, and then shape it the way you would the beaded ring.

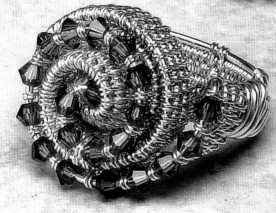

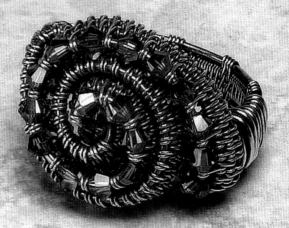

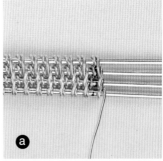

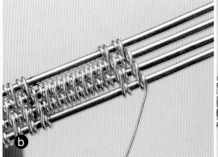

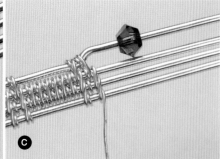

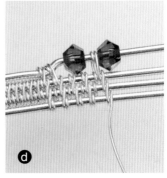

Skills to review:
**filing, p. 18, over-over
weave, p. 40**

Tools

- Weaving tools
- Finishing tools and supplies
- Patina tools and supplies (optional)
- Ring mandrel with a holder
- Hand file
- Plastic or rawhide mallet

Materials

- 40–48 in. 20-gauge dead-soft wire
- 16–18 ft. 28-gauge dead-soft wire
- 18–20 3mm bicone crystal beads with holes large enough (.8mm) to accommodate 20-gauge round wire

Prepare the frame wires

1 Cut the 20-gauge wire into four equal pieces. Line the wires up and tape them together at one end.

2 Find and mark the centerpoint of the wire bundle, and then measure and mark half of your band measurement on either side of the centerpoint. (For a size 5–6½ ring, the band will be 2½ in.; for size 7–8½, 2¾ in.; for size 9–10½, 3 in.; and size 11–12½, 3¼ in. For example: If you are making a size 7 ring, your band will be 2¾ in.; therefore, you will measure 1⅜ in. on either side of the centerpoint.) Next, measure and mark 2½ in. toward the taped end.

Weave the ribbon

3 Work off the spool. Leaving a 12-in. tail, start weaving at the mark closest to the taped end. Weave with the simple four-wire over-over weave for 2½ in. or until you reach the first ring band mark **(photo a)**.

NOTE:
You are leaving a long tail in case you need to add more length to the ribbon when you shape the ring.

---

4 Continue weaving with the same wire, switching to a repeating pattern of six weaves across the two middle wires and two weaves across all four wires **(photo b)**. Weave the entire length of the ring's band section with this pattern, making sure you end with two weaves across all four wires. Don't trim the wire.

5 Make space for the beads: Bend one of the outside frame wires out at a 45° angle. Place the flatnose pliers about 1/16 in. from the bend, and bend the wire again so that it runs parallel to the other wires. String a bead on the bent wire; make sure that it slides on easily and there is no gap between it and the rest of the wires **(photo c)**. Adjust the spacing if necessary. String 19 beads on the wire, and make a small loop at the end of the wire to keep the beads from sliding off.

6 Weave twice across the three bead-free wires. Slide two beads up to meet the weave. Weave once across all four wires, placing the weave between the two beads **(photo d)**.

NOTE:
The second bead is there to help keep the spacing even **(photo d)**.

---

7 Weave twice across the three bead-free wires, slide another bead up, and weave once across all four wires, placing the weave between the second and third bead. Continue this pattern—two weaves across three wires, slide a new bead up, weave across all four wires—until all the beads are used. End with a weave or two across all the wires **(photo e)**. Trim the weaving wire, leaving a 12-in. tail.

Shape the ring

8 Place the ring mandrel in a holder, making sure that the ring size designations are at the top where you can see them. Starting on the underside of the mandrel, position the ribbon so its centerpoint lines up with the number on

the mandrel one size larger than the desired finished ring. Bring both ends of the ribbon up and around the mandrel until they pass each other at the top. Make sure the beaded side of the ribbon is on the inside **(photo f)**.

9 Twist the ribbons around each other, making sure that the first bead ends up in the middle of the knot **(photo g)**. Shift the ribbon slightly if necessary.

10 Start the knot flat; as you continue to spiral, let the inner edge of the ribbon rise up, keeping the outer edge resting against the ring's band. Make the wraps very tight. Go around the full circle twice, ending with the ribbons flat against the ring's band on either side of the ring **(photo h)**.

11 The weaving on the ribbon on either side of the ring should end at the farthest edge of the band **(photo i)**. If either of the woven sections is too short to reach that far, add some extra length to it using the 12-in. tails of weaving wire. If the woven sections are too long, unravel some of the weave. On the beaded side, you may have to add or remove one or two beads. When finished, wrap the ends of the weaving

wire around a frame wire a couple of times and trim.

12 Remove the ring from the mandrel. Working on one side of the spiral, wrap all four ends of the frame wires twice around the ring's band, ending the wrap on the outside of the band. Mark across the wires just inside the edge of the band (so that after they are trimmed, the ends do not extend beyond the edge) **(photo j)**. Lift the ends slightly, and trim them at the mark. Using the flat side of a file, angling it toward the ring's band, carefully file the cut ends. Using flatnose pliers, push the ends tightly against the band **(photo k)**. Repeat for the other side of the ring.

Finish the ring

13 Replace the ring on the ring mandrel and slide it up to the desired size. If necessary, tap the side of the ring with a plastic or rawhide hammer to make it move up. Gently hammer the band to give it a nice, round shape (avoid hitting the crystals).

14 Apply liver of sulfur solution (optional). Tumble for 20 minutes or longer.

Bead Tapestry *necklace*

Looping with beads is a great way to add color to your designs, especially when you mix a bunch of them together in a bold statement necklace. This project gives you a lot of artistic freedom. Not only will you be putting together your own color palette, but you will also create a design for the decorative curlicue end-wires, so that the entire piece will become a one-of-a-kind art piece. The necklace in this project is very large. If you would like to make a smaller version, simply use thinner wires, make the frame smaller, and use smaller beads for the tapestry.

Skills to review:
balling up wire, p. 19, stitching, p. 22, adding wire in looping, p. 22, over-over weave, p. 40, looping with beads, p. 71

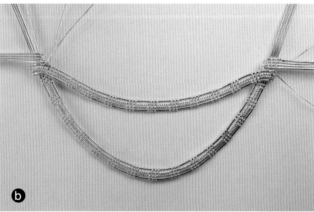

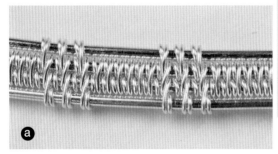

Create the frame

1 Cut the 18-gauge wire into eight 12-in. pieces, and then arrange them into two four-wire ribbons. Starting about 3 in. from the wire ends, weave a 6-in. section of each ribbon with 26-gauge wire. Use an over-over weave with a pattern of three weaves across all four wires and six weaves across the two middle wires **(photo a)** (or choose your own pattern).

2 Shape the ribbons into arcs: Make one almost a semi-circle, and form the other into a gentle curve. Lay them out on the table, both curves turned up with the ends overlapping. The top ribbon's woven section should extend about ½ in. beyond the overlap on either

end. Wrap the ends of the top ribbon around the ends of the lower one where they overlap **(photo b)**.

NOTE:
You can either start at the front and wrap toward the back **(photo c)**, or start underneath and wrap toward the front **(photo d)**. Tape the joins so that the ribbons stay in place as you work on the beaded part of the necklace.

Prepare the bead mix

3 Select beads in three or more complementary colors. Vary the sizes.

Tools
- Weaving tools
- Hot tools
- Finishing tools and supplies
- Patina tools and supplies (optional)

Materials
- 8 ft. 18-gauge dead-soft wire
- 26-gauge dead-soft wire
- 60–80 4–8mm beads
- Chain and clasp

Pour the beads inside the frame of the necklace to see what they will look like all mixed together. You can take a picture to refer to as you work on your bead tapestry **(photo e)**.

Create the beaded center

4 Work with 2–3-ft. pieces of 26-gauge wire. Finish them off, and start new ones as necessary. Decide which side will be the front of your necklace, and keep that side toward you at all times as you loop. Start looping around the inner rim of the frame, adding a bead to each loop. Make sure the beads are close together. Loop all the way around the inside of the frame **(photo f)**. Try to make it look like

the bead placement is random, but also pay attention to the design and color combinations. You want to achieve an organized-chaos effect.

5 In the second row, place an empty loop around each bead. When you get to the point where beads forming adjacent sides meet, connect the two sides by threading the wire through the empty loop around the bead on the opposite side, and then continue to loop around the bead on the side you are currently working **(photo g)**.

6 In the third row, add a bead to each loop again **(photo h)**. In the fourth row, place an empty loop around each third-row bead.

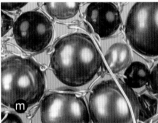

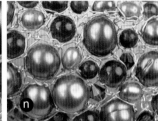

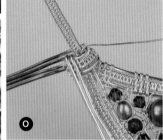

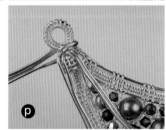

7 After the fourth row, you will probably only have a very narrow space left in the middle—not enough for another complete row of beads all around. At this point, start adding beads, one at a time **(photo i)**, and loop around each individual bead as you go along **(photos j, k)**. Make connections as in step 5. Continue adding beads until there is no space left in the middle.

8 At this point, if you are happy with the way your tapestry looks, finish off the wire. If you have large gaps around some beads, use another piece of 26-gauge wire to weave in between and around the beads to close up the gaps **(photo l, m, n)**.

Create loops for the chain attachments

9 Working on the left side, separate the four frame wires pointing straight up into two sets of two wires each. Bend the two inside wires down until they lie flat against the frame of the necklace. Using basic over-over weave, weave ¾ in. on the two wires still sticking up **(photo o)**. Make a small loop with the woven section.

Separate two wires from the four pointing to the left, and use them to wrap once around the base of the loop **(photo p)**. Repeat for the right side of the necklace.

Make wire curlicue designs

10 Use the ends of the wires to create a nice arrangement of loops and curlicues to fit below and around the loops. You can let some of the longer wires run along the top and bottom of the frame of the necklace. Trim the wires as necessary and ball up the ends **(photo q)**.

11 Use stitching techniques to secure the curlicues to the frame and one another **(photo r)**.

Finish the necklace

12 Attach a chain and a clasp. Apply liver of sulfur solution (optional), and tumble for 20 minutes.

Cabochon

ring

To me, the ultimate test for any jewelry-making technique is whether it can be used for creating a setting for a cabochon. I am thrilled that in wire weaving, there are myriad ways of doing so, some perhaps still unexplored. In this project, you will discover a way to combine a simple over-over ribbon, a looped net, and a curlicue wire that results in a beautiful method for securing a cabochon.

1 Cut the 18-gauge wire into a 10-in. and a 12-in. piece. Mark the centerpoints of the 16- and 18-gauge (10-in.) wires. Mark 5 in. from one end of the 12-in. wire. Line up the marks, and place all the wires together into a flat bundle with the 16-gauge wire on one side, the 12-in. 18-gauge wire on the other side, and the 10-in. 18-gauge wire in the middle. Measure 1⅛ in. from either side of the marks (half the circumference of your stone plus ⅛ in.). Cut an 8-ft. piece of 28-gauge wire (or work off of the spool). Weave the section between the 1⅛-in. marks using over-over weave with a repeating pattern of two weaves across all three wires and 15 wraps on the middle wire. Start and end with one or more weaves across all three wires. Do not trim the weaving wire **(photo a)**.

2 With the 16-gauge wire to the outside, shape the woven section around the cabochon to create a frame. Make sure the ribbon remains flat as you go around. The centerpoint of the ribbon should line up with the middle of one of the long sides of the stone. The frame needs to fit snugly around the stone. Where the wires cross, bend the two inside wires up and out of the way. Bend the other four wires so that they run parallel to each other **(photo b)**.

3 Figure out the length of your ring's band: A size 6 band is about 2¼ in. long. Add ⅛ in. for each size up and subtract ⅛ in. for each size down. For example, the band for a size 8 ring will be 2½ in. long. Mark your ring band's length across the four wires. To get the right length, start the measure at the far side of the inner edge of the

frame. Trim the two outside wires 1 in. and the two middle wires ¾ in. beyond the length of the band. Ball up each wire end **(photo c)**.

4 Continue with the weaving wire from step 1, and weave the length of the ring's band using a repeating pattern of four weaves across the two middle wires and one weave across all four wires. End with one or more weaves across all four wires. Using 2 ft. of 28-gauge wire, loop around the inside edge of the frame. Loop all the way to the center **(photos d, e)**.

5 Center the cabochon on top of the looped area and secure it in place with tape. Using the longer of the two wires that were bent out of the way in step 2, make a small loop at the base and push it against the side of the stone **(photo f)**.

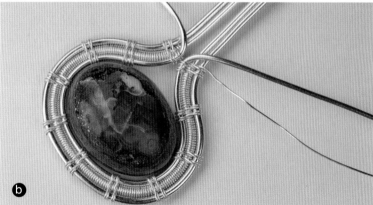

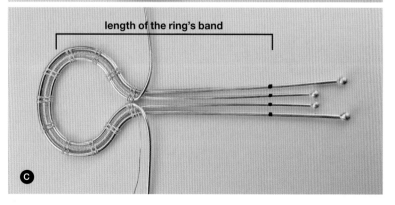

length of the ring's band

Skills to review:
balling up wire, p. 19, stitching, p. 22, over-over weave, p. 40, looping, p. 71

Tools
- Weaving tools
- Hot tools
- Finishing tools and supplies
- Patina tools and supplies (optional)
- Ring mandrel with a holder
- Plastic or rawhide mallet

Materials
- 10 in. 16-gauge dead-soft wire
- 22 in. 18-gauge dead-soft wire
- 12–15 ft. 28-gauge dead-soft wire
- 16x20mm cabochon, about 2 in. circumference

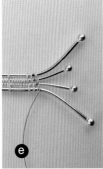

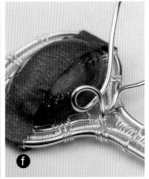

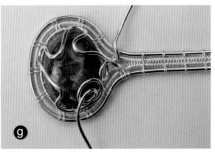

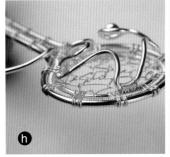

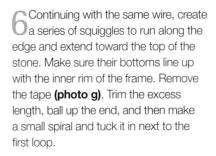

10 Shape the ring around a ring mandrel at a point about 3 sizes smaller than your finished ring will be. At this point, you just need the band to go all the way around and meet the frame **(photo j)**.

11 Use 28-gauge wire to attach the tops of the large loops to the inner edge of the frame on the underside of the ring **(photo k)**.

6 Continuing with the same wire, create a series of squiggles to run along the edge and extend toward the top of the stone. Make sure their bottoms line up with the inner rim of the frame. Remove the tape **(photo g)**. Trim the excess length, ball up the end, and then make a small spiral and tuck it in next to the first loop.

7 Attach the bottoms of the squiggles to the inner edge of the frame **(photo h)**.

12 Place the ring back on the mandrel and hammer it with a plastic mallet to give it a round shape. Push it up the mandrel as far as it will go, and hammer again. Take the ring off, flip it around, and put it back on the mandrel. Hammer again. Repeat, pushing the ring up, hammering, and flipping it until it expands to the correct size. Carefully hammer the woven frame around the stone to make it conform to the shape of the ring band **(photo l)**.

NOTE:
You can remove the stone when working on the first two attachments. Replace it to complete the piece.

NOTE:
Don't rush. This process will put a lot of stress on the wired joints. If you go slowly and take several steps instead of forcefully pushing the ring up the mandrel, the wire will stretch and not break.

---

8 Ball up the end of the shorter wire and wrap it around the ring's band two or three times. Create a loop next to the last wrap, and then bring the balled-up end toward the edge of the frame and attach it to the frame **(photo i)**.

13 Apply liver of sulfur solution (optional). Tumble for 20 minutes or longer.

9 Make symmetrical loops with the wires at the end of the ring's band.

Winged
pendant

The pendant in this project is a great example of how several different techniques can be blended to create a beautiful freeform design. The frame of the pendant is made using over-over ribbon; the bezel holding the cabochon is designed with beaded loops; and the bail and the wings are fashioned out of over-under leaf and crescent silhouettes.

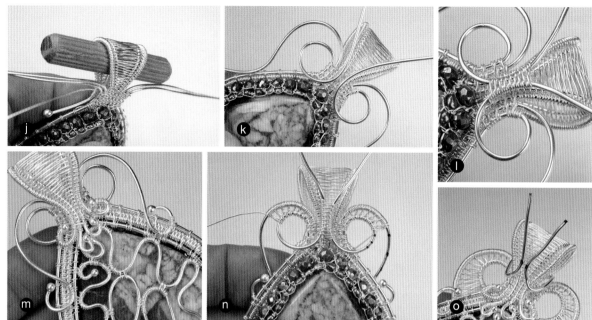

Make the wings and the bail overlay

12 Shape the wires on either side of the bail as shown **(photo k)**.

13 To create the bail overlay, weave together the two wires that come together in the center of the bail. Use about 4 in. of 26-gauge wire and the over-over technique **(photo l)**.

14 Trim the ends of the other two wires 1 in. from where they come in contact with the pendant frame. Ball up the ends, make small spirals, and tuck them into the back of the pendant. Shape the bail wire ends into small spirals; stitch them to the frame **(photo m)**.

15 Weave the wings: Cut two 30-in. pieces of 26-gauge wire (one for each wing). Start weaving at the end closest to the bail. Notice that the wings are crescent shapes with one arc larger than the other. To make the weave, follow the curve evenly, adding extra wraps between weaves on the larger arc (see p. 28 for tips) **(photo n)**.

NOTE:
Weave the two wings simultaneously, switching back and forth.

---

16 Bend the bail overlay wires to run between the bail and the wings, then bring them to the back of the pendant **(photo o; back view)**.

17 In the back: Bend the wires up and toward one another. Mark where they touch, then trim both ends ¾ in. from that mark. Ball up the ends, reshape them, and stitch them together with a few over-over weaves. Make small spirals with the balled-up ends, and press them tightly against the back of the bail **(photo p; back view)**.

18 Use a round-barrelled plastic pen to create a curve in the top the bail: Hold the pen firmly, and press down on the weave while rolling the pen from side to side. Do this for the entire length of the bail from front to back **(photo q)**.

19 Use method #3 for stitching on beads, p. 23, to attach a 6mm bead to the wires at the top of the bail overlay **(photo r)**.

Finishing

20 Apply liver of sulfur solution (optional). Tumble for 20 minutes.

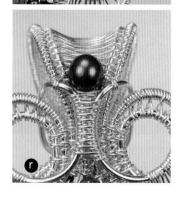

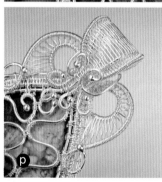

Harmony
one-of-a-kind pendant

Tutorials rarely include insight into an artist's creative process, which is so important to readers who wish to go on to create their own designs after learning the techniques in a book. This final project is a small glimpse into that process, as well as my attempt at showcasing the wilder, more unpredictable side of freeform weaving. My goal with any one-of-a-kind design is to let it evolve organically, allowing it to grow and change through all the stages of the design—from the initial idea all the way to the end of the construction phase. When successful, the resulting piece should look effortless, as if it happened naturally.

I selected a few stones that are considered valuable (bottom) and several that are considered inexpensive (top).

Inspiration

Inspiration can come from many different sources. Nature, music, and art are the obvious ones. What artist would not be awed by a crimson sunrise, a flower in perfect bloom, or a beautiful painting? Conversely, there are many imaginative artists who are also inspired by things that we would normally consider plain and ordinary, such as discarded tires at a junk yard, or screws and washers in a hardware store. They see these objects as more than they appear to be on the surface and picture them alive with a new purpose. Anything can become your inspiration, depending on what moves you and what you find fascinating.

Ideas

Ideas come from inspiration, and good ideas can come at any time. I often find myself desperately searching for a scrap of paper in my purse when I am out and about and something, such as an interesting scroll in a wrought-iron fence, pulls at my creative string. When an idea pops into my head, I want to jot it down immediately, lest it be forgotten. It's a lesson I never learn but maybe you can: Carry a small sketchbook with you at all times!

Not all ideas are spontaneous. Often they have to be coaxed out to play. When I feel uninspired, sometimes just flipping through jewelry books and magazines,or looking through my sketches is enough to get my creative juices flowing. Other times, I doodle on a piece of paper, brainstorming different shapes until something interesting appears.

My favorite thing is to pull out my collection of stones and beads and start playing with them, assembling different configurations until I come up with an arrangement that speaks to me.

A lot of my designs are based purely on visual cues—the balance of shapes, textures, and colors— there is no other hidden meaning, and that is usually enough. However, a design can also be a reflection of an abstract idea, such as a belief or a concept, or it can be based on a theme like nature, architecture, trees, cats, musical instruments, etc.

This project is shaping to be a conceptual one. For a while now, I've wanted to create a design that pairs elements normally considered to be on opposite sides of a spectrum, like an "ordinary" garden-variety pebble and a "valuable" precious stone. The idea came from thinking about how people like to label everything as good/bad/beautiful/ugly/important/ unimportant/valuable/worthless… and how random and subjective the reasons for these labels often are. I was thinking about the link between opposites and the notion of "ugly" being "beautiful" (or vice versa), depending on a situation or a point of view. And so here I will have a "plain" and cheap river stone live together in harmony with a "beautiful" (and much more expensive) precious stone.

Design

I usually start the design process with a list of preset or required elements that have to be included in the design. For this pendant, I need to create a double-stone pendant framed in silver wire; my design must incorporate two stones, silver wire, stone settings,

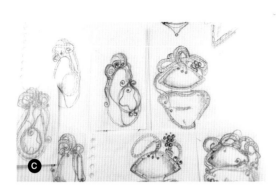

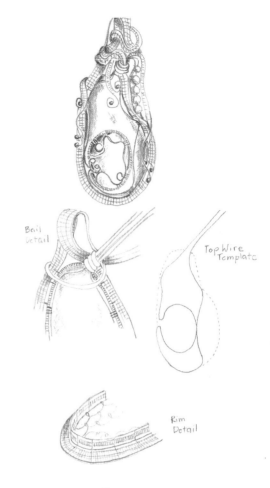

figure

and a bail. These are the preset elements. Having too many of them can stifle the creative process, but a few can be helpful by narrowing the scope of the project and providing a platform that the rest of the design can spring from. From here, I can go on to decide what stones to use, their shapes, colors, and sizes, their position in relation to one another, the method for setting them, the wire, the weave patterns, the overall shape of the pendant, the size and style of the bail, and anything else that may come up while designing and crafting the pendant.

I start by selecting stones that support the concept of my design **(photo a)**. Next, I move the stones around trying different two-stone combinations. As I do this, I visualize each pair as part of the total design with the woven frame around it. If I am lucky, I will come up with something that I can be really excited about. Here, I end up with two pairings that I like a lot, and I have a hard time deciding which one to use **(photo b)**. After doing a few sketches **(photo c)**, I finally decide to develop the pairing on the left because I feel it will end up being a more interesting design. I also like the challenge of coming up with a frame construction for the layered stones.

Sometimes, after selecting the stones, I just pick out some wires and start weaving, making up the design as I go along. However, with a more complex project, it's always a good idea to do a drawing or two to get a better sense of the design's direction and to help work out some of the technical issues such as connections between stones and bezel construction. I like to do my drawings full-scale. I arrange the stones on a piece of sketch paper and then trace around them with a pencil. When I remove the stones, I can draw the rest of the design between and around the traced outlines.

Since the stones have already been selected, and their orientation and relationship to one another decided, the rest of the design is all about the woven frame. Designing the frame, as well as selecting

wires and weaves for its construction, is a fine balance between the functional and the artistic. The functional has to be addressed first—or at least in conjunction with the artistic. As I work on the drawing, I concentrate on the mechanics of the design, keeping in mind the aesthetics. My goal is to figure out methods for attaching the stones that will be secure and visually interesting, and the construction of the bail that will fit the rest of the design and serve as an attachment for a chain.

I may do just one drawing or a whole lot of them **(figure)**. Here, I draw a general sketch of what I want the pendant to look like. Based on that sketch, I decide I need a couple detail drawings to help me figure out the mechanics of the frame and the bail. I also draw a full-scale outline of the top wire of the frame that I will use as a template to shape the wire. At this point, I also make the decision about gauges of wires and weave patterns for the main frame. Based on the sizes of the stones, I will be using 18- and 20-gauge frame wires and 26- and 28-gauge weaving wire.

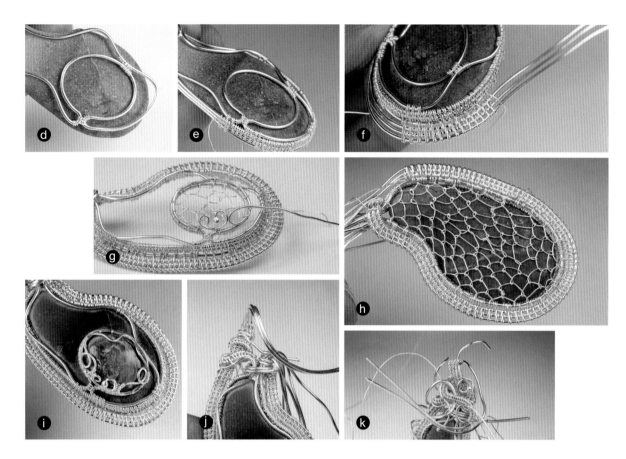

Construct the pendant

I will use the drawings I made as a guide when constructing the pendant. However, the design process continues all the way to the end. I can make modifications at any time.

1 First, I mold the top wire using the template I made earlier. I decide to add small weaves in a few places to keep the shape together **(photo d)**.

2 To make the frame, I cut enough frame wires so that, when stacked, they are the same width as the thickness of the stone. The length of my wires equals the circumference of the stone plus about 10 in. The extra 10 in. will give me 5 in. on either side for the bail. I start weaving at the bottom center of the stone and weave in both directions toward the top. As I weave, I shape the frame using the stone as the template. I adjust the molded top wire as necessary and weave it into the frame in places where it and the frame come in contact **(photo e)**. Notice that the weaving pattern I chose for the frame leaves the lowest wire mostly bare. This makes room for the weave that will attach the rim to the frame in the next step.

3 I cut three 15-in. wires to use as the rim to be woven onto the bottom wire of the frame. I start at the middle bottom of the pendant and weave toward the top, shaping the rim wires as I go and making attachments at equal intervals **(photo f)**.

4 After completing the rim, I am done with the main frame. Next, I weave a piece of 20-gauge wire onto the oval shape that will support the opal cabochon. The wire is about 2½ times as long as the circumference of the opal. Later, I will use the extra length for the squiggle that will hold the stone in place. Even though the cabochon will sit against the larger stone, I decide to add backing (looping) for extra security **(photo g)**. Then I insert the pebble into the main part of frame and permanently secure it in place by closing the back with loops **(photo h)**.

5 I insert the opal into its frame and shape the extra piece of wire from step 4 to create a squiggly border and attach it to the frame with stitching techniques **(photo i)**. At this point, the main part of the pendant is complete, and the next step is to fashion the bail and any ornamental additions.

6 Using my sketch as a reference, I shape the bail **(photo j)**. Once the bail is woven, I start arranging and weaving the wires around it to create a pleasing design that will complement the rest of the pendant **(photo k)**.

Gallery

▼ Amber Crystal Cuff, 2011
Fine silver wire, Swarovski crystal
Photo by Jerry Anthony

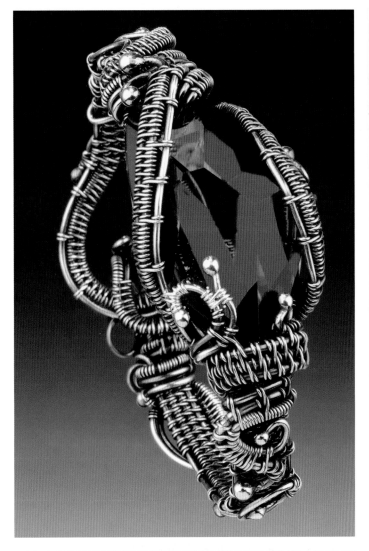

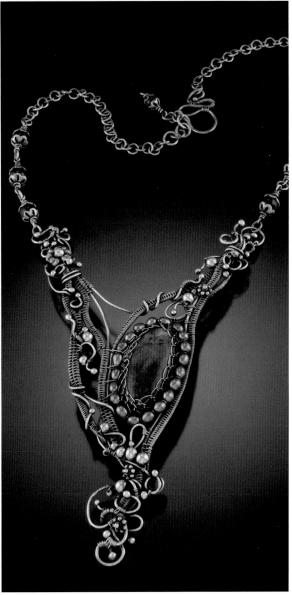

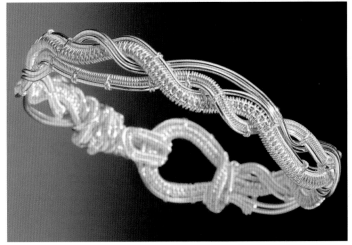

**◄ Braided
Bracelet, 2011**
Fine silver wire
Photo by Jerry Anthony

**▲ Autumn Wind
Necklace, 2012**
Fine silver and sterling silver wire,
Ohio flint, freshwater pearls
Photo by Larry Sanders

▼ Butterfly Wing Cuff, 2012

Fine silver wire, butterfly wing jasper, various beads

Photo by Larry Sanders

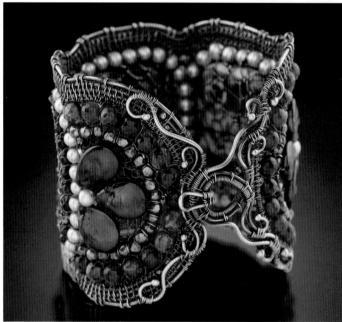

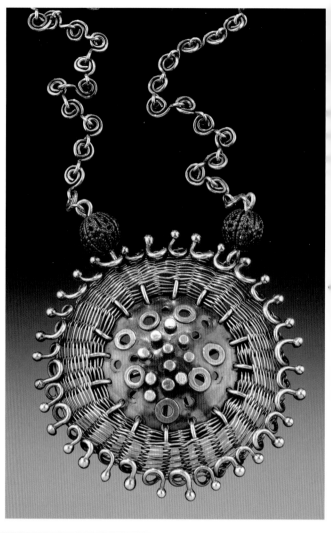

▲ Desert Flower Necklace, 2011

Fine silver and sterling silver wire, copper

Photo by Jerry Anthony

◄ Coiled Collar Necklace, 2009

14k gold-filled wire, freshwater pearls

Photo by Kaska Firor

▼ Forest Fairy Necklace, 2012

Fine silver, moss turquoise, beads
Photo by Larry Sanders

➤ Watermelon Tourmaline Pendant, 2011

Fine silver, watermelon tourmaline
Photo by Kaska Firor

▲ Three Sisters Pendant, 2011

Fine silver wire, boulder opal, Oregon opal, quartz
Photo by Jerry Anthony

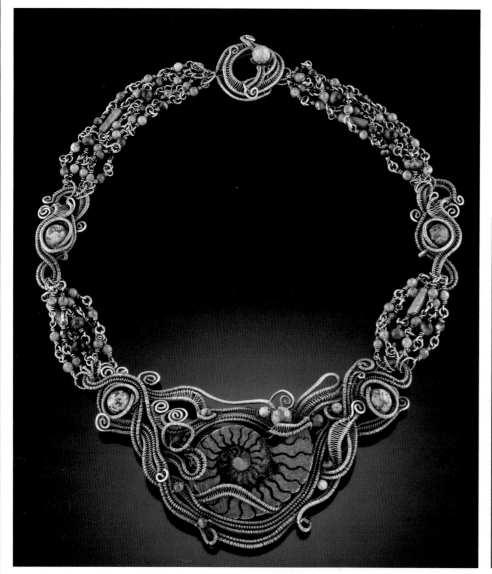

◀ **Fossil Necklace, 2009**
Sterling silver wire, ammonite fossil, beads
Photo by Larry Sanders

▲ **Lady in Green Necklace, 2012**
Fine silver and sterling silver wire, prehnite, opal
Photo by Larry Sanders

◀ **Bead Tapestry Necklace 1, 2009**
Sterling silver wire, various beads
Photo by Jerry Anthony

▲ **Tiger Eye Pendant, 2009**
Sterling silver wire, tiger eye
Photo by Kaska Firor

About the Author

Kaska Firor graduated from the University of Cincinnati with a BA in Interior Design. Over the years, her love of handcrafts led her to pursue other creative avenues as well, including clay sculpture, stained glass, sewing, and eventually wire arts. She has been designing and crafting wire jewelry since the summer of 2000, when she took her first instruction in that medium. She spent several years working with traditional wire-wrapping techniques honing her skills and experimenting with various types of wires and tools.

In the last few years, her focus has shifted to more innovative wire techniques, including those borrowed from basket weaving and textile arts. The intricate and visually complex patterns of the weaves originally attracted Kaska to wire weaving, and her fascination with the art continues to grow as she discovers more complex and challenging ways of combining and modifying different techniques and more inventive ways of incorporating stones, beads, and other elements into her woven designs.

Kaska displays and sells her jewelry at art shows in the Midwest, where she has won numerous awards. Her work has been published in several trade magazines; most recently, her woven bracelet design was featured on the cover of March 2012 issue of *Art Jewelry* magazine. She teaches jewelry classes locally at her studio in Cincinnati, Ohio, as well as nationally. She believes that strong foundations are the key to successful design. In her classes, she emphasizes proper technique and attention to detail and challenges her students with projects designed to increase their skill level.

Let your wirework imagination *soar!*

Spotlight on Wire

Learn to twist, fold, hammer, weave, and wrap your way through 25+ unique projects for all skill levels! Innovative techniques for woven wire, corrugated wire, textured wire, and more create results typically achieved only with expensive equipment.

64377 • $21.95

Build Your Own Wire Pendants

Making beautiful pendants is as easy as 1 • 2 • 3 with Kimberly Berlin's clever mix-and-match method! Learn to make a basic frame and bail, add interest with embellishments, and interchange techniques to create a one-of-a-kind piece every time.

64568 • $19.95

Lacy Wire Jewelry

Create the delicate, airy look of filigree wirework without soldering! Easy techniques provide exciting options for twisting and sculpting wire into 30 projects that include earrings, pendants, necklaces, pins, bezels, hair jewelry, and more.

62939 • $21.95